PAPER MONSTERS
& CURIOUS
CREATURES

WITHDRAWN

PAPER MONSTERS
& CURIOUS
CREATURES

30 PROJECTS TO COPY, CUT, AND FOLD

CAMILLUS

Hiroshi Hayakawa

LARK

An Imprint of Sterling Publishing
387 Park Avenue South
New York, NY 10016

ISBN 978-1-4547-0783-7

Library of Congress Cataloging-in-Publication Data

Hayakawa, Hiroshi, 1962-
  Paper monsters & curious creatures / Hiroshi Hayakawa.
    pages cm
  Includes index.
  ISBN 978-1-4547-0783-7
  1. Paper animal making. I. Title. II. Title: Paper monsters and curious creatures.
TT870.H3824 2014
745.592--dc23
                              2013043161

Distributed in Canada by Sterling Publishing
c/o Canadian Manda Group, 165 Dufferin Street
Toronto, Ontario, Canada M6K 3H6
Distributed in the United Kingdom by GMC Distribution Services
Castle Place, 166 High Street, Lewes, East Sussex, England BN7 1XU
Distributed in Australia by Capricorn Link (Australia) Pty. Ltd.
P.O. Box 704, Windsor, NSW 2756, Australia

For information about custom editions, special sales, and premium and corporate purchases, please contact Sterling Special Sales at 800-805-5489 or specialsales@sterlingpublishing.com.

Email academic@larkbooks.com for information about desk and examination copies.
The complete policy can be found at larkcrafts.com.

Every effort has been made to ensure that all the information in this book is accurate. However, due to differing conditions, tools, and individual skills, the publisher cannot be responsible for any injuries, losses, and other damages that may result from the use of the information in this book.

Manufactured in China

2 4 6 8 10 9 7 5 3 1

larkcrafts.com

PAPER MONSTERS

& CURIOUS CREATURES

*This book is
dedicated to Nanette,
the most impressive
dreamer I know.*

INTRODUCTION

We all enjoy being scared and entertained by monsters and curious creatures. Frankenstein's Monster, Dracula, Mummy, Wolfman, Medusa, Invisible Man ... the list goes on. We marvel at the fertile human imaginations that brought those creatures to life. In the course of everyday life, I often stop and wonder what kinds of secrets this universe still has in store for us. Who can say with absolute certainty that Big Foot or the Loch Ness Monster doesn't exist?

Those monsters and curious creatures are so deeply embedded in our childhoods and have so thoroughly permeated our popular culture that they've practically become part of who we are. Their stories make our lives richer because they are reflections of us, only highly dramatized and goose-bump-inducing reflections. They show us what's good and what's bad about ourselves and teach us a lesson or two.

This book will give you a chance to invite these wonderful creatures back into your life in a very creative way. It contains many fun and frightful projects you can make out of paper. It's filled with monsters, space aliens, robots, and other creatures from books, TV, movies, myths, and legends. They all have tons of personality, but don't worry—they really aren't all that scary. Some of them are actually kind of cute in their own way!

All the projects in this book were designed using two types of traditional paper craft techniques: origami and kirigami. In Japanese origami means "paper folding," and kirigami means "paper cutting." In this book, I will show you how to combine these two techniques to create monsters that are three-dimensional and full of details. The techniques involve three very distinct processes: scoring, cutting, and folding. Most of the projects have interlocking joints that give them enough structural strength to stand alone without the use of adhesive. Some projects and accessories require a little bit of glue.

Before you pick up a pair of scissors and start cutting, however, read the section called How to Use This Book (page 7). The process for making each monster is the same: Photocopy or print the project template and follow the step-by-step instructions and illustrations to score, cut, fold, and shape it into a dimensional (and expressive) monster. Some of the projects might look a bit intimidating at first, but you'll discover that the process of carefully shaping paper is actually quite simple and even meditative. So familiarize yourself first with the basic steps, and then begin creating.

The projects in this book are grouped by skill level: easy, intermediate, and advanced. If you are new to kirigami, I suggest you start with the easiest projects before you work your way up to the more complex ones.

Designing these creatures was so much fun. My imagination went wild and worked overtime—just like Dr. Frankenstein in his laboratory! I hope you enjoy making these monsters and curious creatures as much as I enjoyed designing them. Perhaps this book will awaken the little monsters hiding inside of you.

Hiroshi Hayakawa

HOW TO USE THIS BOOK

You might think that creating 30+ monsters and curious creatures out of paper would require quite the collection of techniques and tools, but the reality is rather simple: Each of these projects is made by scoring, cutting, folding, and shaping paper, and you'll need only a few basic tools to get going! This section of the book thoroughly explores basic kirigami techniques as well as some tips to help you along the way. The projects' step-by-step illustrations and templates include symbols that explain where to cut, fold, and so on, and you'll find a descriptive explanation of those symbols in the following pages.

WORKING WITH THE TEMPLATES

Every project in this book begins with a full-size template, found on pages 99 – 128. Keep in mind that the template details are meant to be printed on the reverse side (or underside) of your paper: Make sure you score and cut on the printed side. Once you've constructed the monsters, most of the printed folding lines won't be visible on their outer surfaces.

Photocopy the templates instead of using the originals. This way, you will be able to make as many of each monster as you like. Why not construct a whole family of mummies? Loch Ness Monster might be lonely without a girlfriend. You can make dozens of paper skeletons for Halloween decorations. You'll also find templates for accessories, including an axe for Minotaur, a broom and pointed hat for the Wicked Witch, and a sickle for the Grim Reaper.

PAPER

Creating dimensional paper projects requires paper thin enough to be easily folded yet sturdy enough to give structural strength to the finished pieces. With this in mind, you'll need to copy the project templates onto cardstock rather than regular printer paper. All of the projects in this book were made with cardstock, which you can easily find at your local office supply or craft store.

You can choose from a variety of cardstock thicknesses, colors, shades, and textures. Stay away from inexpensive cardstock that may have a white core in the center. When you score and fold such paper, the white core will appear in your fold.

To photocopy or print on cardstock, adjust the printer's paper setting. Depending on your printer, you may want to hand feed the cardstock one sheet at a time to avoid jamming.

SYMBOLS

As you work on the projects, you'll need to understand the symbols that appear on the templates and in the illustrations that come with the assembly instructions. These are shown and described below.

A transition from one step to the next

Move a part of the template or a tool in the direction of the arrow

Movement occurs toward/on the reverse side of the template

Turn over a part of the template, reversing the inside/outside relationship

Create a rounded surface with your fingers or by rolling it over a dowel

Create a curved surface with a dowel. The shape of the arrow indicates the general shape and the direction of the curve.

Enlarged view of a smaller section

Indicates ups and downs of the surface levels after a series of folds

Turn over the entire template

SCORING

Scoring is the act of creating lines and edges in paper that will facilitate folding and shaping. Scoring is the first step in making any of the projects (yes, even before cutting out a template). You'll score the folding lines first, which are indicated by dashed and dotted lines on a template.

Scoring makes folding easier and neater later on. If you cut out the template first, scoring these lines, especially in a small, delicate area, is sometimes more difficult, so it's best to score first.

Begin by placing the template on a smooth, flat, hard surface. A surface that's too soft, such as newspaper, may cause you to dig deep grooves into the template as you score, which would make the assembled project unsightly.

The key to successful scoring is to avoid exerting too much pressure on your scoring tool. Score the folding lines with an awl, a small nail, a bone folder, a ballpoint pen that's run out of ink, or anything else with a hard, pointed tip. **(A)** Even though some of the scored lines will be folded downward and others will be folded upward, score them all on the same printed side of the template. Try not to stray from the marked lines.

To make scoring straight lines easier, use the edge of a ruler as a guide. **(B)**

CUTTING

After you've scored the folding lines, you'll begin cutting. The solid lines on the templates represent the cutting lines.

First, use a craft knife to cut along all the solid lines within the interior perimeter of the template. These lines include small cuts along the eyes, the opening of the nose for some of the projects, and the cutting lines of the tabs for interlocking joints. When making small, curved cuts such as those for the eyes, rotate the paper in the opposite direction as the movement of your knife. **(C)**

Be very careful when using a craft knife. Keep your hand away from the path of the blade. A small child may need an adult's help when making precision cuts.

Next, use a pair of scissors or a craft knife to cut along the contour perimeter of the template. **(D)**

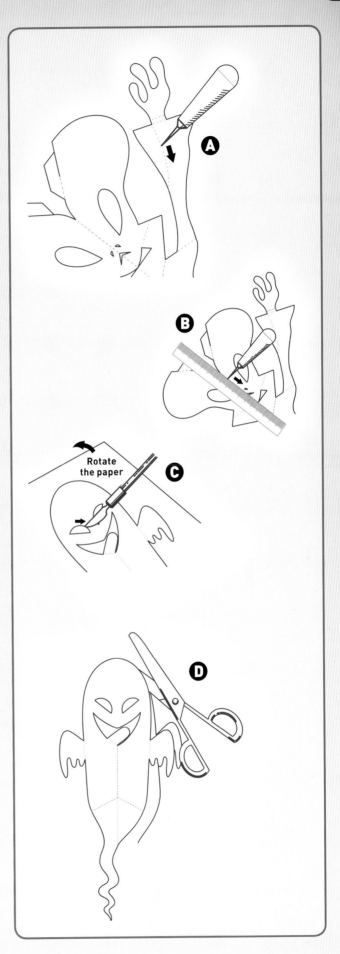

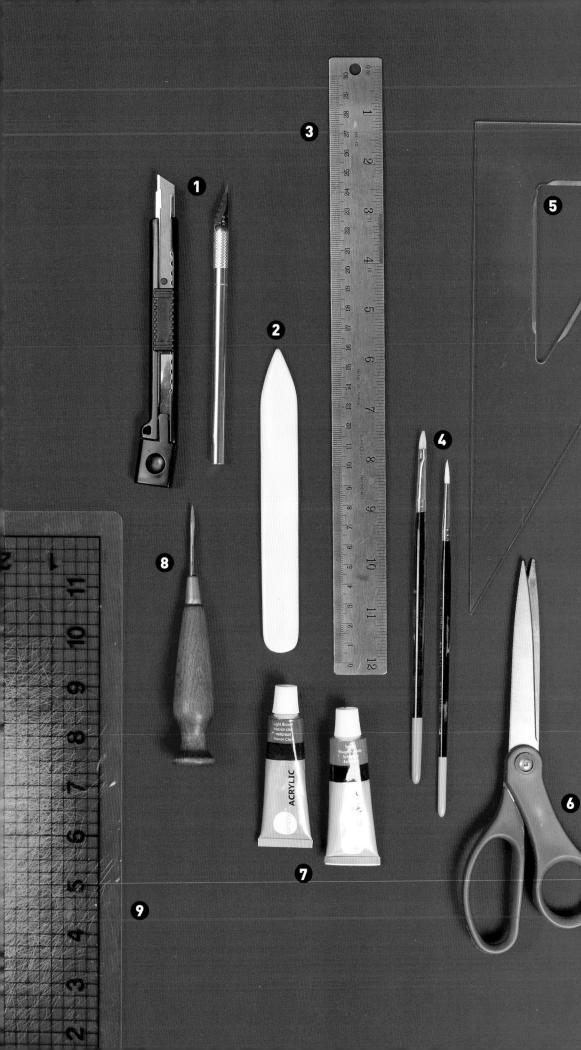

TOOLS

1. Craft knives
2. Bone folder
3. Ruler
4. Thin brushes
5. Triangle ruler
6. Scissors
7. Paint
8. Awl
9. Cutting board

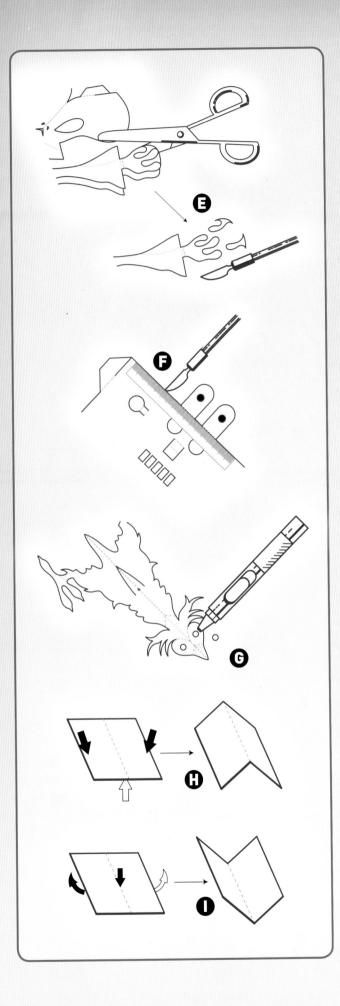

When cutting away small, sharp areas that extend beyond the template's contour but toward the interior (the Space Alien's hand shown at the left is a good example), first use scissors to make a rough cut, and then cut away the remaining paper with a craft knife, moving the instrument from the interior toward the exterior. **E**

Cutting a straight line is easy. Use the edge of a ruler as a guide—the same as when you are scoring a straight line—and cut along the line with a craft knife. Use a metal ruler so that you don't damage its edge with the blade. **F**

To cut out small circles, such as the eyes of the Phoenix (Phoenix project is available free at larkbooks.com/bonus), you can use a craft knife, but the best tool for this job is a paper (or a leather) punch. **G**

Select a tip of the right size, align the tip of the punch with the circle you are cutting out, and gently tap the end of the tool with a wooden or rubber mallet.

FOLDING

Now that you've scored and cut out the project template, you'll begin the really fun part: folding. This is when the monster or creature actually starts to take on the shape of a dimensional object. Two types of folds are used in this book: the peak fold and the valley fold. A peak fold is represented by a dotted line, a valley fold by a line of dashes. Most folding can be done with your fingers, but small, delicate sections will require a little help from some tools.

Making a Peak Fold
Use the index finger and the thumb of one hand to push down on both sides of the dotted line, while simultaneously pushing up the area under and along the folding line with the index finger of your other hand. **H**

If the section of the template that calls for this type of fold is too small for the edge of your finger, use a small tool, such as a toothpick, a needle, or the awl that you used for scoring.

Making a Valley Fold
Use one finger to push down along the dashed line of the template, while pushing up both sides of the folding line with the index finger and the thumb of your other hand. Again, if the section to be folded is to small for your finger, push down the folding line with a small scoring tool instead. **I**

Folding a Curved Line

To fold a curved line, use your thumb and index finger to pinch and squeeze along opposing sides of the folding line while pushing the area under and along the folding line with the index finger of your other hand. **J**

Making a Pocket Fold

Pocket folding—a combination of a peak fold and a valley fold—is typically used to form the neck-shoulder and tail-hip connections of some of the projects, such as the Loch Ness Monster's neck. The figure below illustrates how to make this fold. **K**

SHAPING

Some of the monsters and curious creatures require the use of a few simple shaping techniques. These techniques aren't applicable to all the projects in this book, but using them adds a sense of realism and character to your work.

The first technique is used to round the body of a project such as Cerberus (Cerberus is a bonus project available free at larkcrafts.com/bonus). After cutting out the template, turn it over. Use one hand to press the template against the edge of a desk or a table and use the other hand to pull it back and forth across the edge a couple of times. This will add a natural curve to the body. **L**

You can create a round or curved surface by shaping a template with your fingers, but for a small area of a template, roll it over a dowel. **M** **N** A dowel produces a much neater result than rolling the template with your fingers. If you don't have a dowel, substitute a round pencil or any other thin, tubular object.

Many of the projects in this book are held together by means of interlocking joints. They make it possible to assemble the monsters without using glue or tape and provide them with enough strength to make them freestanding. **O** When a project is completed, the last step is to adjust the angles of the legs so that the creature will stand comfortably on its feet without falling over.

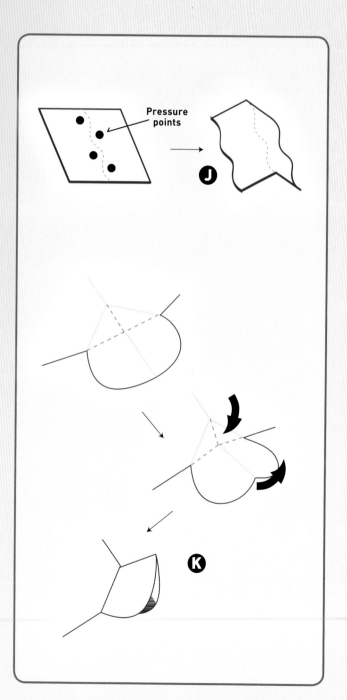

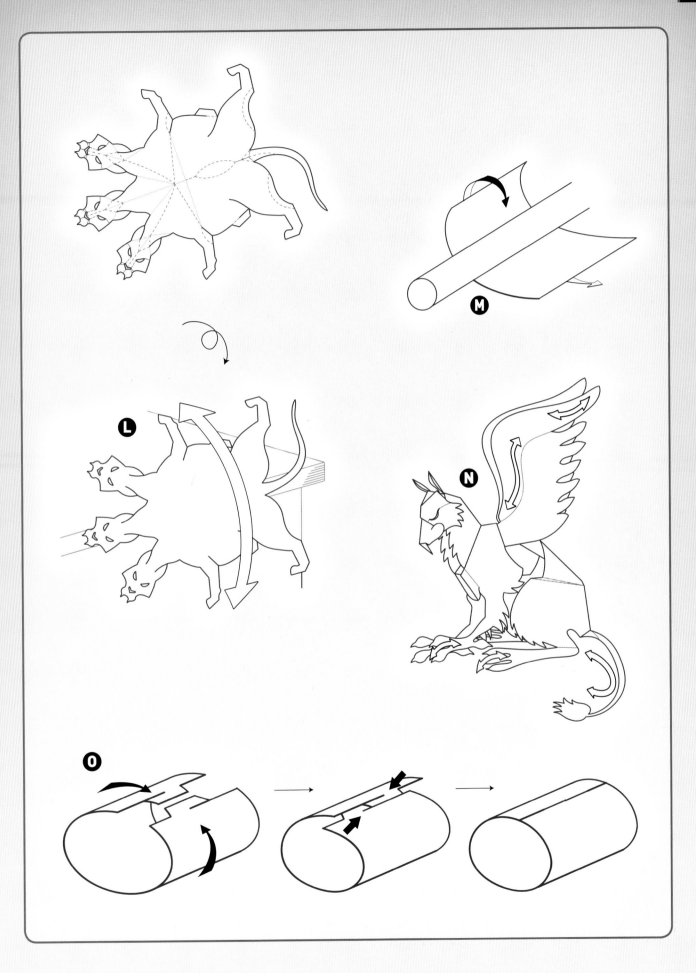

GLUING

Some projects and accessories require a small amount of glue. The parts of the templates where you need to apply glue are indicated in the step-by-step instructions. You can use common white glue, PVA glue, or any craft glue that is water washable. When applying glue to a very small part of the template, I recommend using the tip of a toothpick.

COLORING

Although the coloring of many projects is based on how the monsters are commonly depicted, you don't have to follow the examples in this book. Study the samples in the photographs, but feel free to follow your fancy when applying colors or unusual patterns to the projects—after all, these are fanciful creatures! Perhaps your Invisible Man wants to wear a colorful suit? Or maybe you'd like a pink Mummy? Why not?

You can use any opaque paint or drawing medium, as long as it isn't oil-based. Acrylic paint, tempera, poster paint, colored pencils, and pastels will all work just fine.

SELECTING A PROJECT

The projects in *Paper Monsters and Curious Creatures* range in skill level from easy to advanced, and while they all employ the same basic techniques, it's a good idea to practice a bit before diving right into a challenging or intricate design. If you're new to paper-cutting and folding crafts, or if you are a youngster, I recommend that you get your feet wet with the simpler projects in the easy group and gradually move on to more detailed ones as you practice and develop your skills.

Check out www.larkcrafts.com/bonus for templates and instructions to make these additional monsters, creatures, and accessories:

**BABY ALIEN • BLACK CAT • CERBERUS
CHIMERA • CRAWLING ZOMBIE
GOLEM • MERMAID • NOSFERATU
PHOENIX • SEATED GARGOYLE
TRASH CAN ROBOT • JACK O' LANTERN
HEADSTONE • FLYING SAUCER
DRACULA'S COFFIN**

MONSTERS

DEVIL

DIFFICULTY LEVEL >> **EASY**

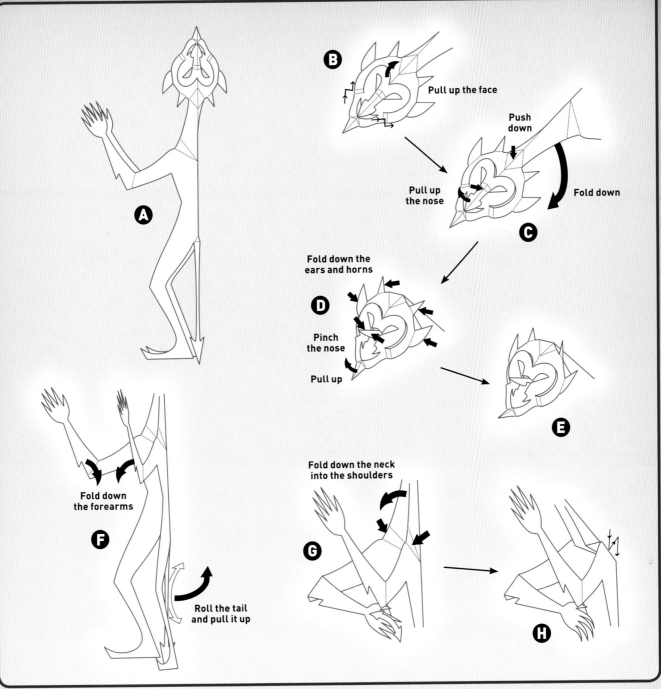

B Pull up the face

Push down

Pull up the nose

Fold down

C

Fold down the ears and horns

D

Pinch the nose

Pull up

E

Fold down the forearms

F

Roll the tail and pull it up

Fold down the neck into the shoulders

G

H

1 Using the Devil template on page 99, score the folding lines. Then cut along all the solid lines, including the eyes, the face, the nose, and the mouth, as depicted in How to Use This Book on pages 7 – 14.

2 Fold the body in half following the scored centerline. Leave the head and the tail unfolded. **A**

3 Pull up the face toward the head following the folding lines at the bottom of the cheeks. **B**

4 Pull up the nose by pocket folding its base into the face. Fold down the neck behind the head while you valley fold the top of the head. **C**

5 Pinch the nose. Pull up the pointed chin by pocket folding its base. Fold down the horns on the head and ears to the front. **D** **E**

6 Fold down the forearms from the elbows. Roll the tail over a dowel to curve it, then pull up the tail from the hips. **F**

7 Fold down the neck into the shoulders to lower the head. Roll the fingers of the right hand over a dowel to curve them. **G** **H**

8 Fold the fingers of the left hand so that it can hold the spear.

9 Add color to your Devil by referencing the project photos.

10 If you want to give your Devil a spear, the template is on page 99.

GHOST

DIFFICULTY LEVEL ≫ **EASY**

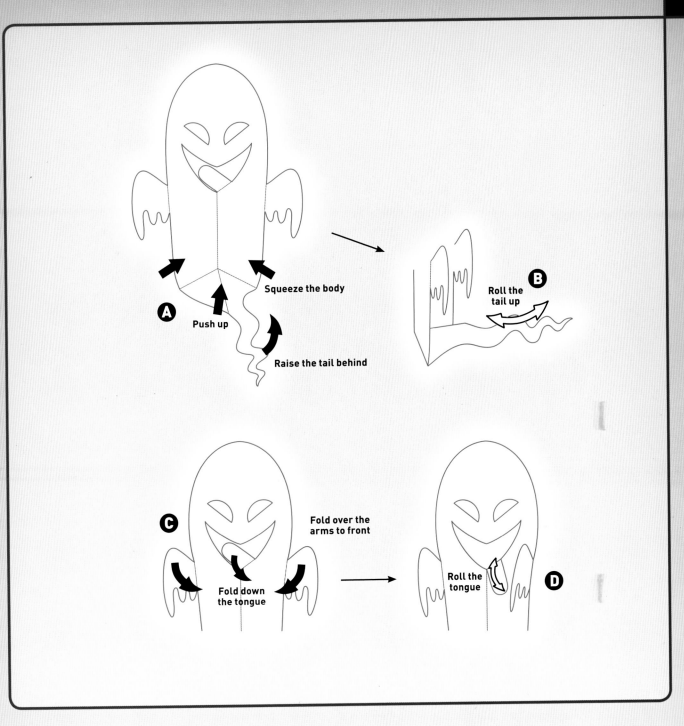

1 Using the Ghost template on page 128, score the folding lines. Then cut along all the solid lines, including the eyes and the mouth, as depicted in How to Use This Book on pages 7 – 14.

2 Squeeze in the hips while pushing up the center of the bottom of the body with your finger from underneath to raise the tail. **A**

3 Roll the tail over a dowel to shape it. **B**

4 Fold down the tongue. Fold over the arms to the front of the body. **C**

5 Roll the tongue over a dowel to curve it. **D**

6 Paint the tongue red. Add any other colors you'd like to your Ghost by referencing the project photos.

LOCH NESS MONSTER

Fold the neck into
the shoulders

Raise the neck

Add curves
to the tail

A

Roll the neck

B

Pull up the
eyelids

Push in the
cheeks

Roll the nose

Shape the
fins

C

D

1 Using the Loch Ness Monster template on page 100, score the folding lines. Then cut along all the solid lines, including the eyelids and the nostrils, as depicted in How to Use This Book on pages 7 – 14.

2 Fold the body in half following the scored centerline. Leave the head unfolded. Pocket fold the bottom of the neck into the shoulders. Add natural curves to the tail. **A**

3 Roll the neck over a dowel to give it a U shape. Shape all four fins by referencing the project photos. **B**

4 Pull up the eyelids and push in the cheeks. Roll the nose over a dowel to make it round. **C D**

5 Add color to your Loch Ness Monster by referencing the project photos.

FRANKENSTEIN'S MONSTER

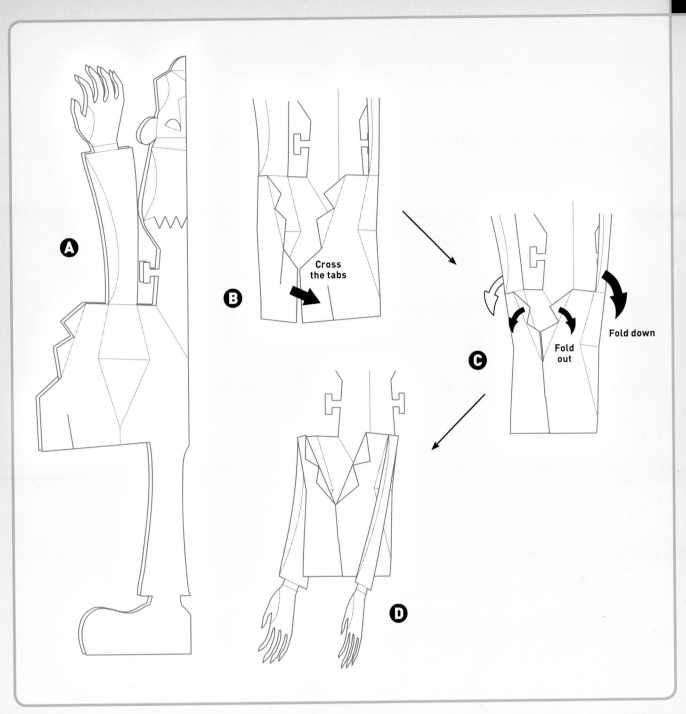

Cross the tabs

Fold down

Fold out

A

B

C

D

1 Using the Frankenstein's Monster template on page 102, score the folding lines. Then cut along all the solid lines, including the eyes, the nose, the hair, and the tabs for the interlocking joint, as depicted in How to Use This Book on pages 7 – 14.

2 Fold the template in half by following the scored centerline. **A**

3 Shape the body by following the folding lines. Cross the tabs for the interlocking joint on the stomach. **B**

4 Fold down the arms and fold out the jacket lapels. **C** **D**

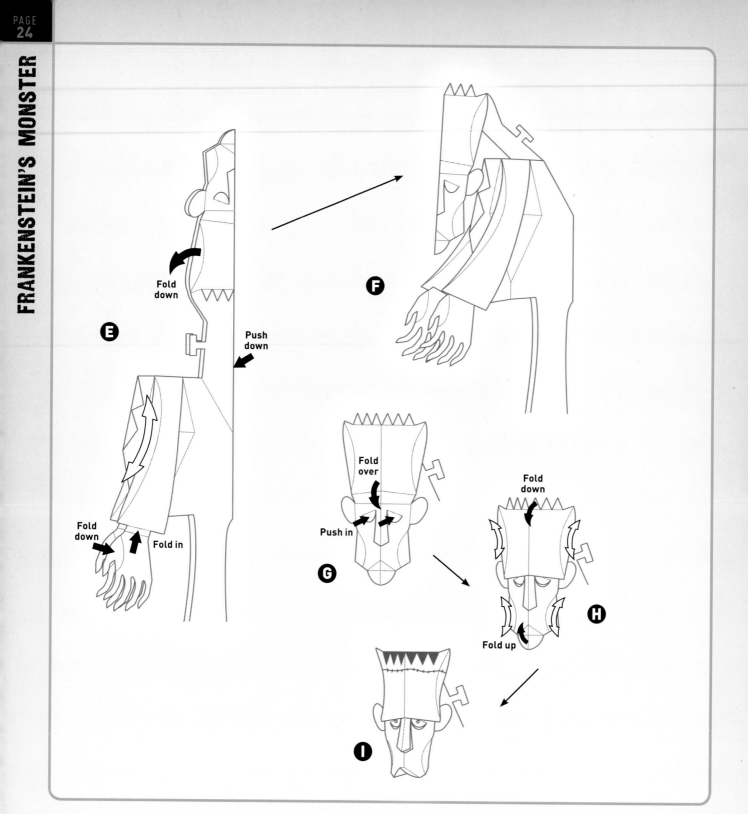

5 Fold the wrists into the sleeves. Fold down the thumbs. Add curves to the arms following the scored lines. Push down the back of the neck and valley fold it into the shoulders while you fold down the head toward the chest from the scored line running across the top of the head. **E F**

6 Fold down the forehead over the eyes. Push the eyes into the sockets. **G**

7 Fold down the hair over the forehead. Pull up the chin by pocket folding it. Shape the forehead and the cheeks by following the folding lines in them. **H**

8 Draw eyes and stitches on the head. Add color to your Frankenstein's Monster by referencing the project photos. **I**

BRIDE OF FRANKENSTEIN

DIFFICULTY LEVEL >> **INTERMEDIATE**

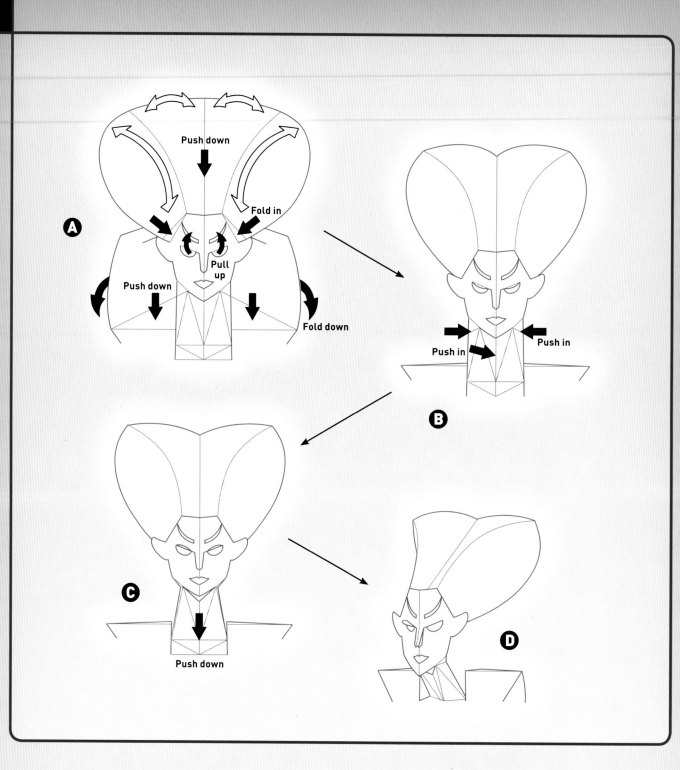

1 Using the Bride of Frankenstein template on page 103, score the folding lines. Then cut along all the solid lines, including the eyes, nose, mouth, eyebrows, the hairline at the top of the forehead, the chin, and the tabs for the interlocking joint, as depicted in How to Use This Book on pages 7 – 14.

2 Start with the head. Pull up the eyelids. Fold in the hair at the temples behind the ears. Roll the hair over a dowel. Push down and valley fold the center of the hair. Fold down the shoulders and the tabs to the back. **A**

3 Push in both sides and the center of the neck. **B**

4 Push down and pocket fold the bottom of the neck into the shoulders following the scored folding lines. When you do this, the head will naturally come forward. **C D**

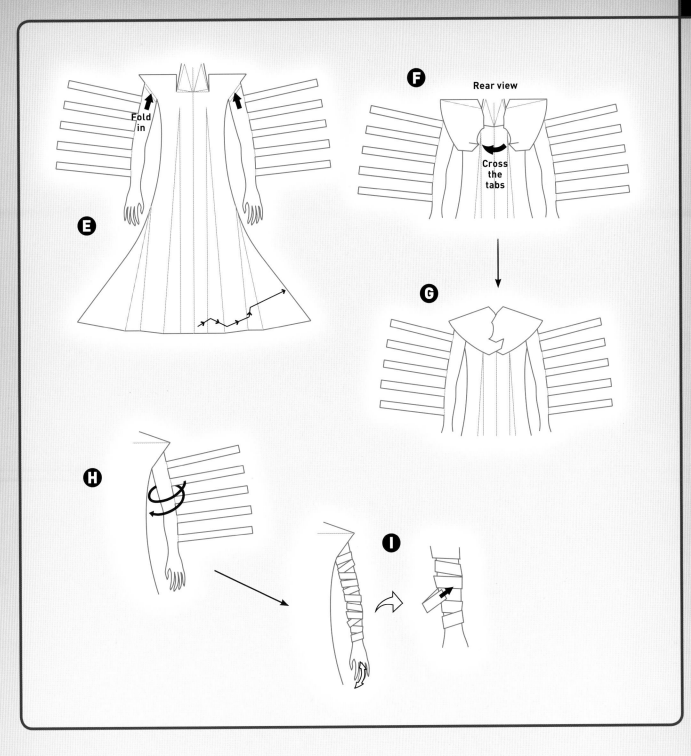

5 Fold the top of the arms into the shoulders. Shape the bottom of the dress following the scored folding lines. **E**

6 Turn over the template. Bring the tabs for the interlocking joint to the center and cross the tabs behind the shoulders. **F G**

7 Wrap the bandages around the arms randomly. **H**

8 Slide the end of the bandage under the part already wrapped to hold the strips in place and to make it look neat. You can also use a small amount of glue for this. Roll the fingers over a dowel. **I**

9 Add color to your Bride by referencing the project photos.

DRACULA

DIFFICULTY LEVEL >> INTERMEDIATE

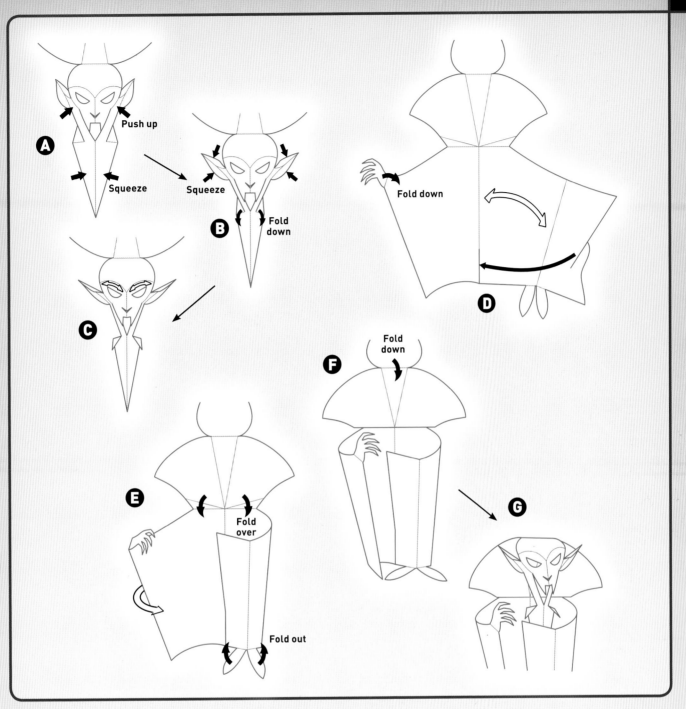

1 Using the Dracula template on page 104, score the folding lines. Then cut along all the solid lines, including the eyes, the nose, the mouth, the collars of the shirt, and the tabs for the interlocking joint, as depicted in How to Use This Book on pages 7 – 14.

2 Start with the head. Push up the cheeks. Pinch and squeeze the chest. **A**

3 Fold down both sides of the collar. Pinch and squeeze the ears following the scored folding lines in them. **B**

4 Shape the eyebrows by folding the curved lines above the eyes. **C**

5 Fold down the hand from the wrist. Round the right side of the cape over a dowel. Bring the tab for the interlocking joint to the center of the body and cross the tab with the cut you made at the bottom of the cape. **D**

6 Fold the collar of the cape over the shoulders. Fold the feet out. Round the left side of the cape over a dowel so that the hand will come up front. **E**

7 Fold down the head and insert the pointed end of the chest into the opening of the cape. **F** **G**

8 Adjust the angles of the feet and the cape so that your Dracula will stand securely.

9 Add color to your Dracula by referencing the project photos.

10 If you'd like to give your Dracula a coffin to sleep in, the template and its assembly instructions are available free at larkcrafts.com/bonus.

GRIM REAPER

DIFFICULTY LEVEL >> INTERMEDIATE

Push up

Fold in

A

N

B

Squeeze in

C

Push down

Fold out

Pull up

Fold down

D

E

Fold back

1 Using the Grim Reaper template on page 105, score the folding lines. Then cut along all the solid lines, including the eyes, nose, mouth, and the tabs for the interlocking joints, as depicted in How to Use This Book on pages 7 – 14.

2 Work on the head first. Fold in the lower jaw under the upper jaw following the patterns of the folding lines. Then push up the entire jaw toward the skull. **A**

3 Roll the two halves of the skull over a dowel to make them round. Bring them closer to the back and cross the tabs for the interlocking joint over the neck. Squeeze in the lower jaw. **B** **C**

4 Pull up the head and fold down both sleeves toward the chest. Fold out the sides of the hood and push down the top. (The head of the Grim Reaper should now be cradled inside the hood.) **D**

5 Fold back the two halves of the cloak. **E**

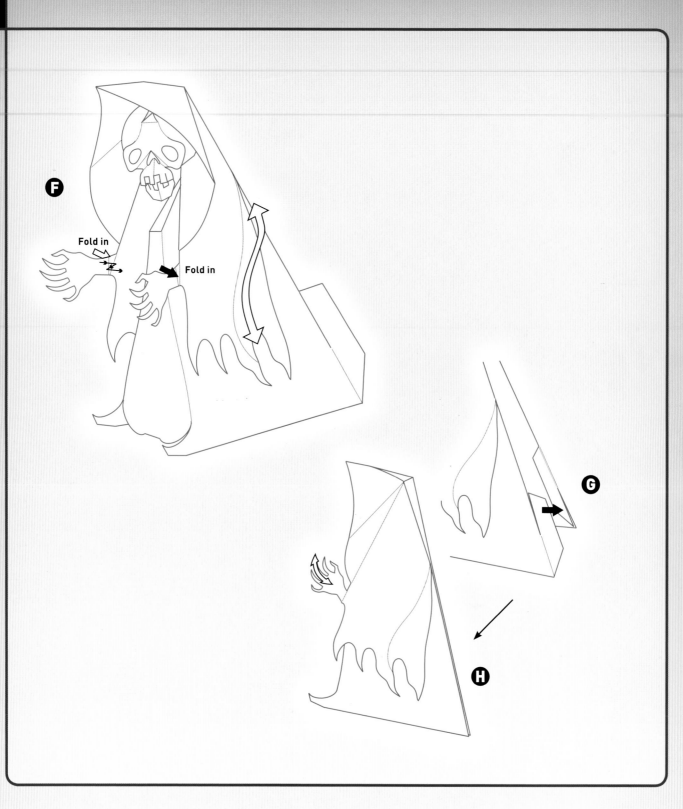

Fold in

Fold in

F

G

H

6 Fold the hands into the sleeves. Shape the sleeves and add wavy curves to them. **F**

7 Cross the tabs for the interlocking joint in the back. Roll the fingers over a dowel to shape them. **G** **H**

8 Add color to your Grim Reaper by referencing the project photos.

9 You can give your Grim Reaper a sickle for his soul hunting. The template is on page 104.

INVISIBLE MAN & DOG

DIFFICULTY LEVEL >> **INTERMEDIATE**

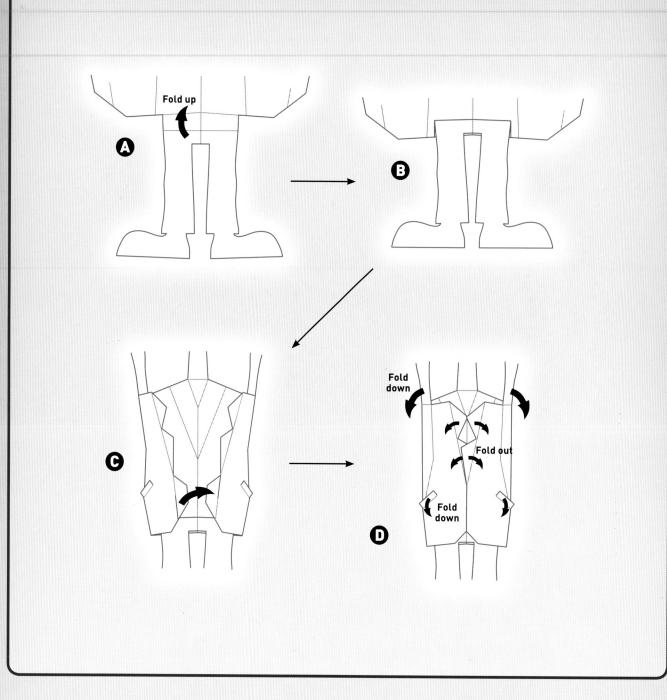

1 Using the Invisible Man template on page 107, score the folding lines. Then cut along all the solid lines, including the glasses, the pockets, and the tabs for the interlocking joints, as depicted in How to Use This Book on pages 7 – 14.

2 Fold the legs and pull them up over the hips. **A** **B**

3 Fold over and close the front of the jacket following the scored lines on the sides. Cross the tabs for the interlocking joint. **C**

4 Fold down the arms. Fold out the lapels of the jacket and the flaps of the pockets. **D**

5 Fold the cuff of the right arm into the sleeve. Fold over and insert the wrist straps into the cuts made in both sleeves. **E** **F** **G** **H**

E **F**

Fold over
and insert

Fold in

G **H**

Fold over
and insert

I

Fold
down

Fold up

Fold down

Fold
down

L

J

K

M

Push in

N

6 Score the folding lines of the Dog Collar template on page 107 and cut it out. Fold up all the studs to raise them. Fold down the leash. Round the collar over a dowel and interlock the joint by crossing the tabs at the ends. **I**

7 Run the left arm through the loop of the leash and insert the end of the arm into the opening of the pocket. **J** **K**

8 Fold down the glasses. Bring down the chin to the shoulders. Round the two halves of the face mask over a dowel. **L**

9 Cross the tabs behind the head and interlock the joint. **M**

10 Turn the template around. Push down the center of the shoulders. **N**

11 Add color to your Invisible Man by referencing the project photos.

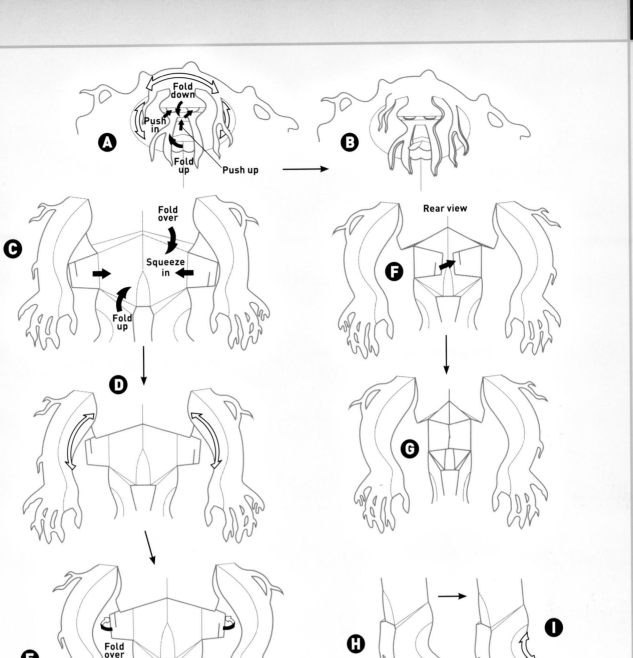

1 Using the Swamp Thing template on page 101, score the folding lines. Then cut along all the solid lines, including the eyes, the lines in the face, and the tabs for the interlocking joint, as depicted in How to Use This Book on pages 7 – 14.

2 Push in the eyes. Fold down the forehead toward the face. Fold up the chin and push up the jaws. **A** **B**

3 Fold the chest over the stomach. Fold up the legs. Squeeze in the stomach. **C**

4 Fold the arms along the scored lines and add curves to them. **D**

5 Fold over the tabs of the interlocking joint on the sides of the body. **E**

6 Turn the template over. Bring the two tabs for the interlocking joint together behind the back and cross the tabs. **F** **G**

7 Fold the feet out to the sides. **H**

8 Shape the legs by folding them along the scored lines. Adjust the angle of the legs so that your Swamp Thing will stand comfortably. **I**

9 Paint the eyes red. Add color to your Swamp Thing by referencing the project photos.

WICKED WITCH

DIFFICULTY LEVEL ≫ INTERMEDIATE

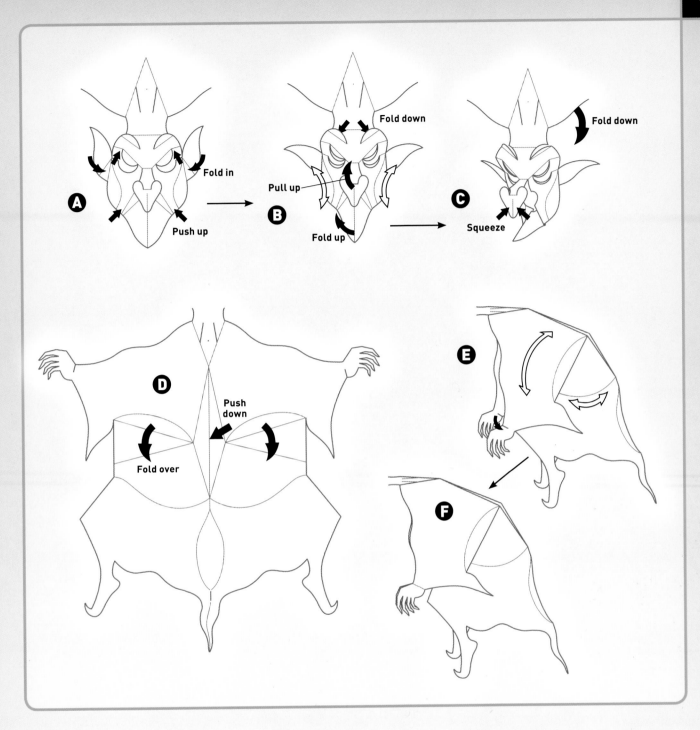

1 Using the Wicked Witch template on page 106, score the folding lines. Then cut along all the solid lines, including the eyes, the nose, the eyebrows, the lines under the eyes, the cuts at the top of the head and the rear end of the body, and the tabs for the interlocking joint, as depicted in How to Use This Book on pages 7 – 14.

2 Fold in the bases of the ears. Push up the eyes and the cheeks. **A**

3 Fold down the eyebrows. Pull up the nose. Fold up the chin. Push in and shape the cheeks. **B**

4 Squeeze the tip of the nose. Fold down the neck behind the head from the line at the top of the forehead. **C**

5 Fold the body of Wicked Witch in half. At the same time, fold the sleeves over the sides of the body and push down the center of the back. **D**

6 Shape the sleeves and the hips by adding curves to them. Then cross the tabs of the interlocking joint of the wrists to put both hands together. **E** **F**

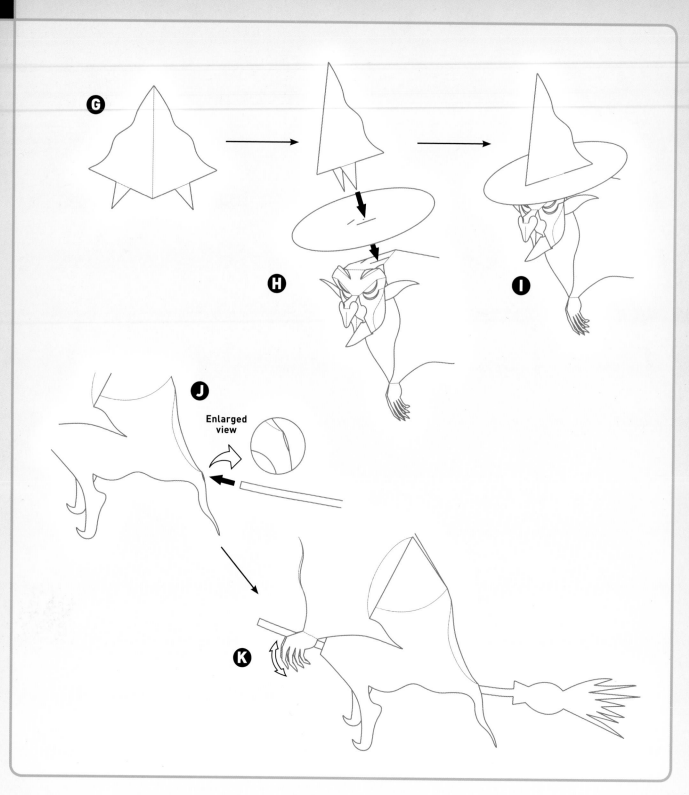

G

H

I

J

Enlarged
view

K

7 Score and cut out the templates for the Witch's hat on page 106. Fold the top of the hat in half. **G**

8 Run the two tongues of the top of the hat through the cuts you made in the disk-shaped bottom piece. Then insert them into the cuts on top of the Witch's head.

Fold the tongues under the head to secure the hat in place. **H I**

9 Cut out the Witch's broom on page 106. Run the top end of the stick through the cut you made in the rear end of the Witch's body. Roll the fingers so that your Witch can hold the broom in her hands. **J K**

10 Draw in the eyes and add color to your Wicked Witch by referencing the project photos. If you want your witch to fly, run thread through the dot at the top of the head and then through the dot in the center of the hat.

DIFFICULTY LEVEL >> **INTERMEDIATE**

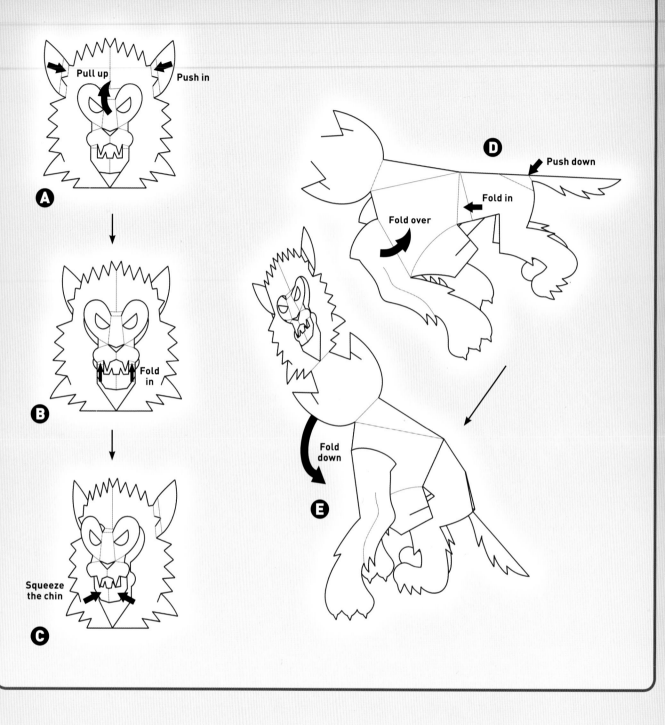

1 Using the Wolfman template on page 108, score the folding lines. Then cut along all the solid lines, including the eyes, the nose, the mouth, the outline of the face, and the tabs for the interlocking joints, as depicted in How to Use This Book on pages 7 – 14.

2 Push in the ears and pull up the face. **A**

3 Fold in the lower jaw and bring up the muzzle. **B**

4 Squeeze the chin. **C**

5 Fold over the arms. Push the lower body into the upper body. Push down the tail and pocket fold it into the hips. **D**

6 Fold down the collar in front of the chest. **E**

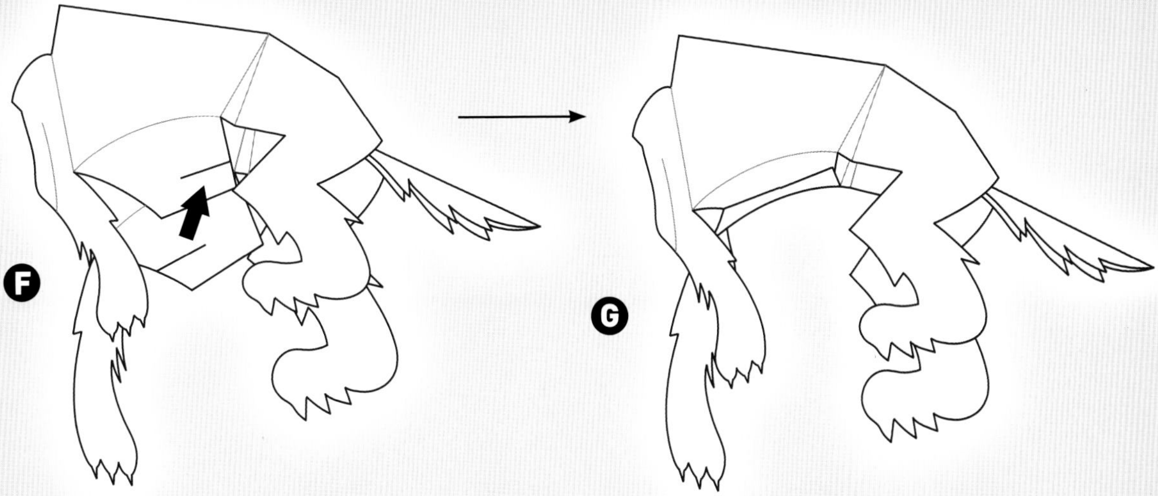

F

G

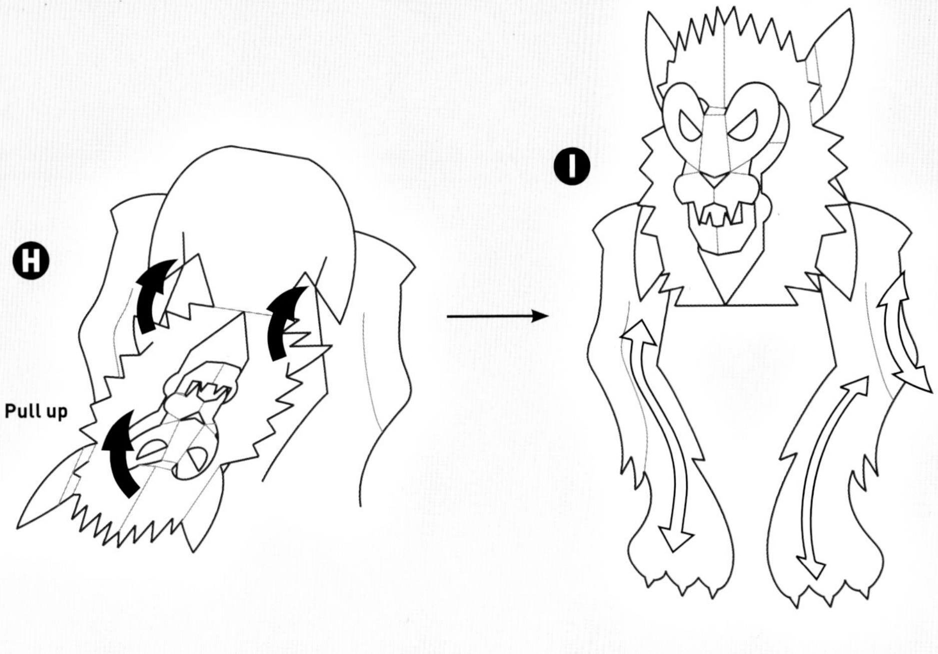

H

Pull up

I

7 Interlock the chest joint by crossing the tabs. **F** **G**

8 Pull up the head and interlock the cuts made into the mane and the ones in the collar so that the head will stay up. **H**

9 Shape the arms. **I**

10 Adjust the angles of the legs and arms so that your Wolfman will stand securely.

11 Add color to your Wolfman by referencing the project photos.

ZOMBIE

DIFFICULTY LEVEL >> **INTERMEDIATE**

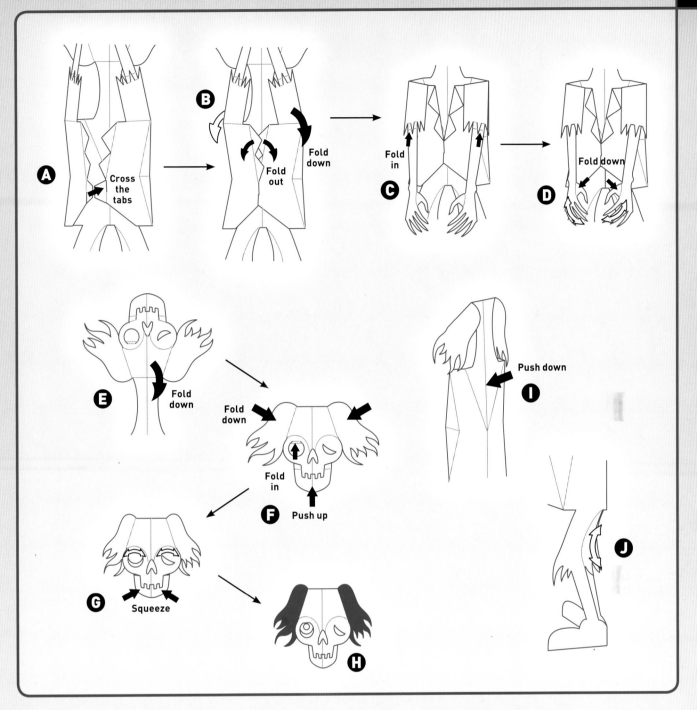

1 Using the Zombie template on page 109, score the folding lines. Then cut along all the solid lines, including the eyes, the nose, the mouth, and the tabs for the interlocking joint, as depicted in How to Use This Book on pages 7 – 14.

2 Shape the body by following the folding lines. Cross the tabs of the interlocking joint on the stomach. **A**

3 Fold down the arms, and fold out the jacket lapels. **B**

4 Fold the arms into the sleeves. **C**

5 Fold down the thumbs. Roll the fingers over a dowel. **D**

6 Fold down the head to the chest. **E**

7 Push up the chin under the teeth. Fold down the hair on the sides of the head. Fold in the eyeball. **F**

8 Pinch and squeeze the lower jaw. Push in and round the upper eyelids. **G** **H**

9 Push down the back of the neck and valley fold it into the shoulders. **I**

10 Shape the back of the thighs following the scored folding lines. **J**

11 Add color to your Zombie by referencing the project photos.

BONUS PROJECT
Crawling zombie available free at www.larkcrafts.com/bonus

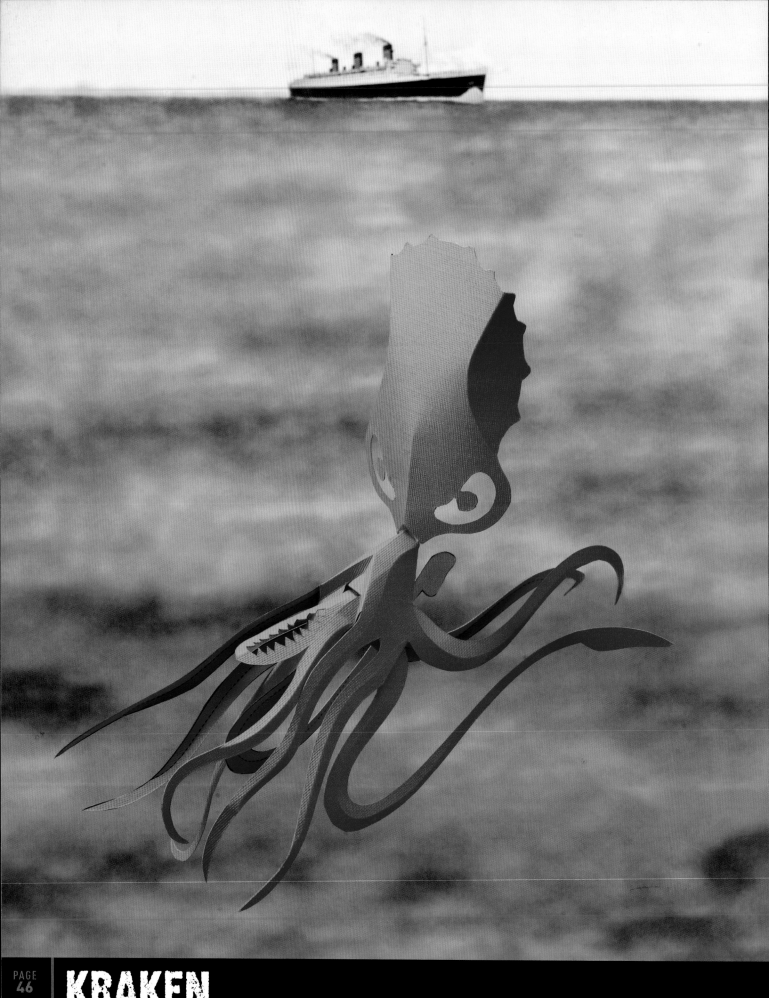

KRAKEN

DIFFICULTY LEVEL ≫ ADVANCED

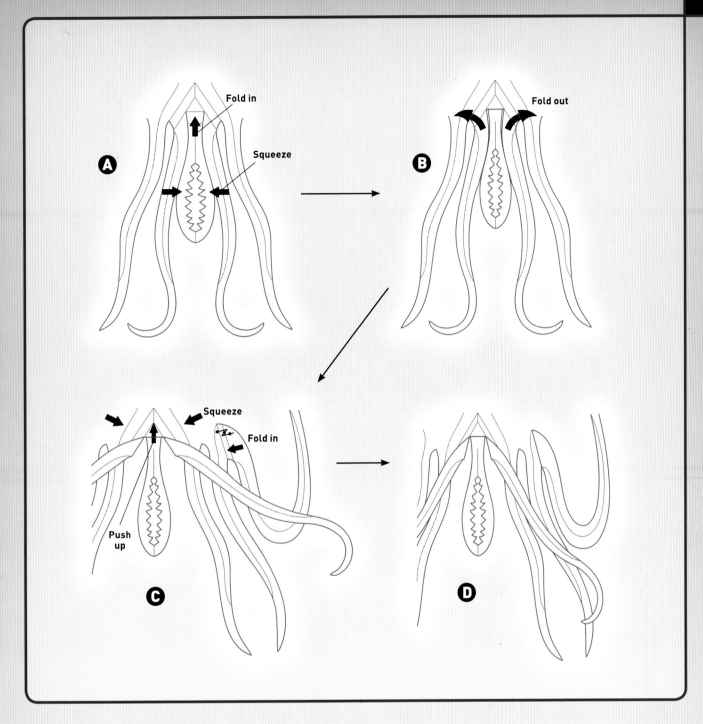

1 Using the Kraken template on page 110, score the folding lines. Then cut along all the solid lines, including the eyes, the mouth, and the tabs for the interlocking joint, as depicted in How to Use This Book on pages 7 – 14.

2 Fold in the mouth under the upper body and squeeze the mouth following the scored centerline. **A**

3 Fold out the two innermost tentacles. **B**

4 Push up the top of the mouth while you squeeze in the base of the tentacles. Fold in the bases of the two arms. **C D**

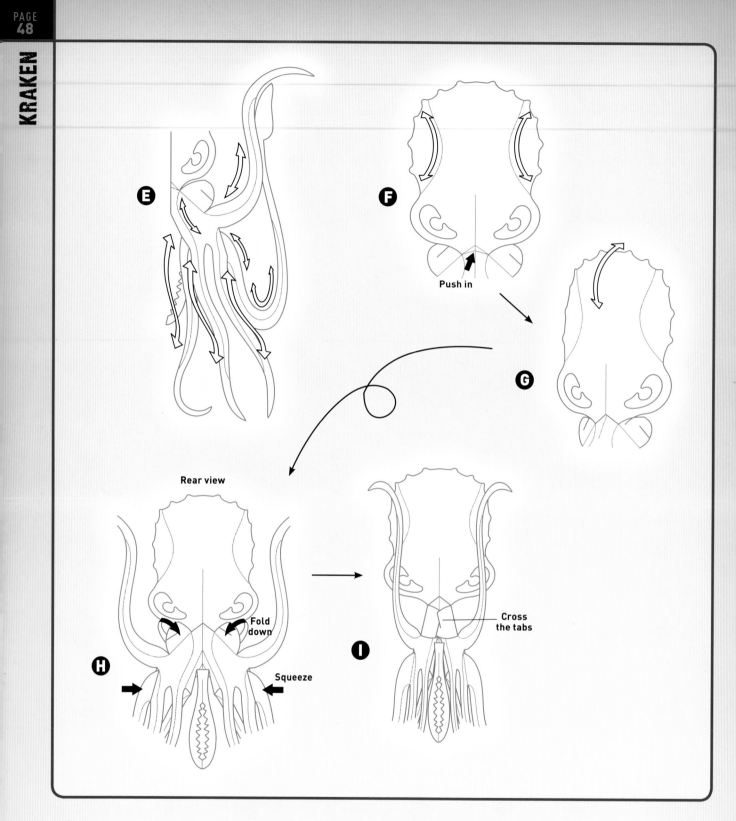

E

F
Push in

G

Rear view

H
Fold down
Squeeze

I
Cross the tabs

5 Shape all the tentacles and arms by following the scored lines in them. **E**

6 Following the scored folding lines, add curves to the sides of the head. Push the top of the lower body into the head. **F**

7 Add a curve to the top of the head. **G**

8 Turn the template over. Fold down the two tabs for the interlocking joint. Squeeze in the entire lower body to create a sort of bundle. **H**

9 Cross the tabs of the joint. Fine-tune and make necessary adjustments to the angles and shapes of the tentacles so that your Kraken will stand comfortably. **I**

10 Add color to your Kraken by referencing the project photos.

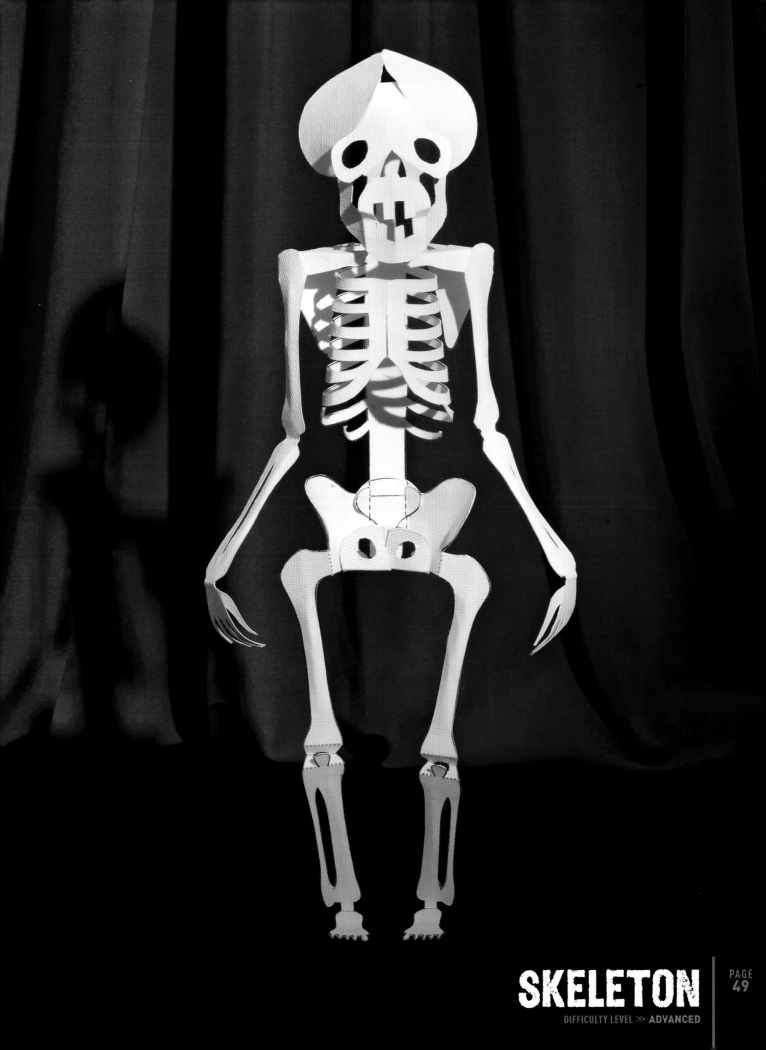

SKELETON

DIFFICULTY LEVEL >> **ADVANCED**

SKELETON

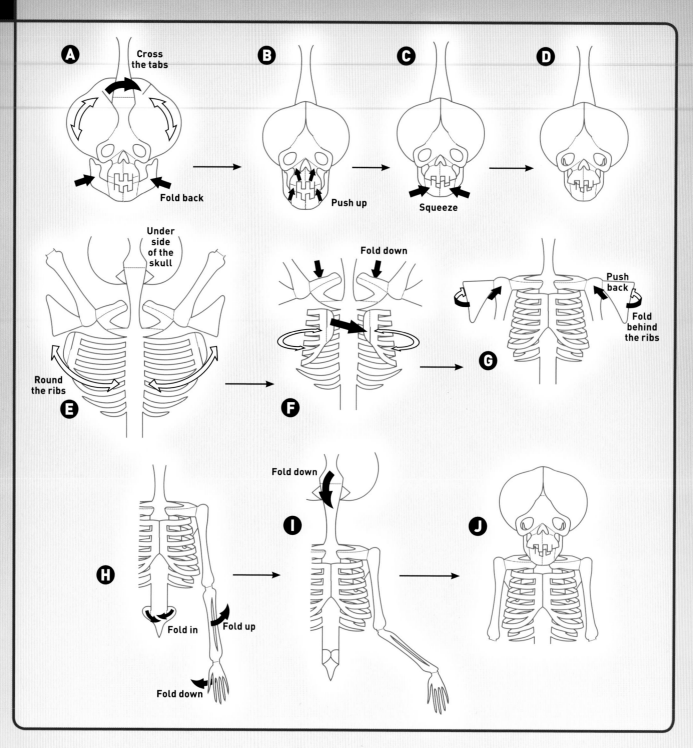

1 Using the Skeleton template on page 111, score the folding lines. Then cut along all the solid lines, including the eyes, the nose, the mouth, the ribs, the cuts in the pelvis, and the tabs for the interlocking joints, as depicted in How to Use This Book on pages 7 – 14.

2 Start with the skull. Fold the outsides of the lower jaw to the back. Round the two halves of the skull and cross the tabs for the interlocking joint over the neck. **A**

3 Push up the upper jaw toward the eyes, then push up the lower jaw. When you do this, the upper and bottom teeth will overlap. **B**

4 Squeeze the chin. **C** **D**

5 Round the ribs over a dowel. **E**

6 Bring the two halves of the rib cage to the center and cross the tabs for the interlocking joint. Fold down the collarbone and bring the arms down following the scored folding lines in the middle. **F**

7 Push back the upper arms to the sides of the ribcage. Fold the shoulder blades behind the ribs so that they will be positioned in the back. **G**

8 Fold up the forearms and fold down the hands. Fold in the flaps of the heart-shaped end of the spine. **H**

9 Fold down the head from the scored folding line at the top of the neck. **I** **J**

Ⓚ Squeeze in

Push back

Cross the tabs

Fold up

Ⓛ Pull up

Fold up

Ⓜ Round the pelvis

Ⓝ Insert

Ⓞ Pull up

Open up

Ⓟ

10 Work on the lower body next. Squeeze in the pelvis and interlock the joint at the bottom of the hips by crossing the tabs. Fold up the bottom of the hips to the front. Push back the thighbones slightly. Ⓚ

11 Pull up the lower legs following the folding lines at the knees. Fold up the feet. Ⓛ

12 Round the pelvis. Ⓜ

13 Insert the bottom end of the spine through the cuts you made in the center of the pelvis. Run it through the first cut at the top from behind, make it come out up front, and then lodge the tip into the second cut at the bottom of the pelvis. Ⓝ

14 Open up the flaps of the spine. Then slightly pull up the spine to securely connect the upper body and the lower body. Ⓞ Ⓟ

15 Add color to your Skeleton by referencing the project photos.

16 If you want to hang your Skeleton, run a thread through the X on the skull. You can also give your skeleton a more realistic look by rounding the leg bones and the arm bones over a thin dowel.

MEDUSA

DIFFICULTY LEVEL >> ADVANCED

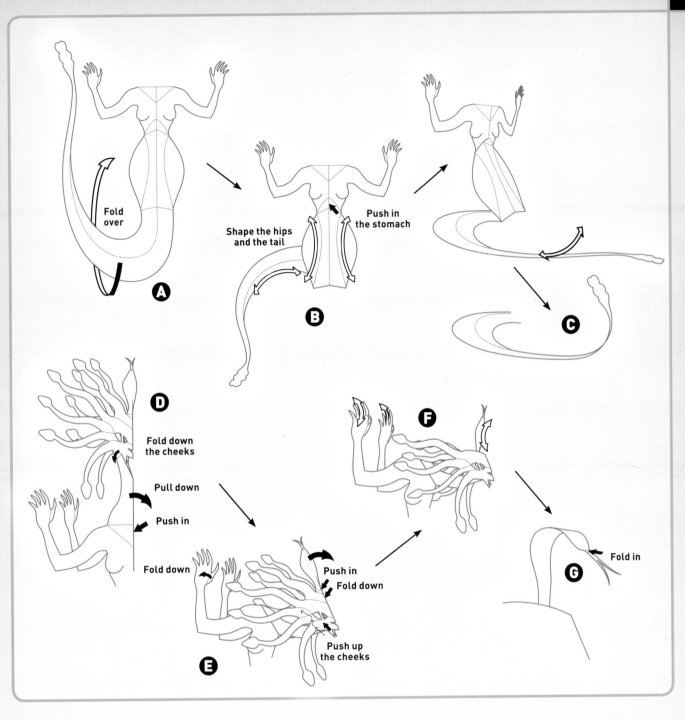

Fold
over

A

Shape the hips
and the tail

Push in
the stomach

B

C

D

Fold down
the cheeks

Pull down

Push in

Fold down

Push in
Fold down

E

Push up
the cheeks

F

Fold in

G

1 Using the Medusa template on page 112, score the folding lines. Then cut along all the solid lines, including the eyes, the mouth, and the nose, as depicted in How to Use This Book on pages 7 – 14.

2 Fold the tail over to the back from the bottom of the body. **A**

3 Push in and pocket fold the stomach. Shape the hips and the tail following the folding lines. **B**

4 Roll the tail over a dowel to make the end curl up. **C**

5 Push in the triangle shape on the neck and pocket fold it into the shoulders. Fold down the cheeks over the top of the neck. **D**

6 Fold down the thumbs into the palms of the hands. Push up the cheeks. Push in the snake on top of the head and pocket fold it into the forehead. Fold down the forehead. **E**

7 Roll the fingers and the snake on the head over a dowel. **F**

8 Fold in the tongue of the snake. **G**

9 Roll and shape all the snakes on Medusa's head to your liking. Add color to your Medusa by referencing the project photos.

MUMMY

DIFFICULTY LEVEL >> ADVANCED

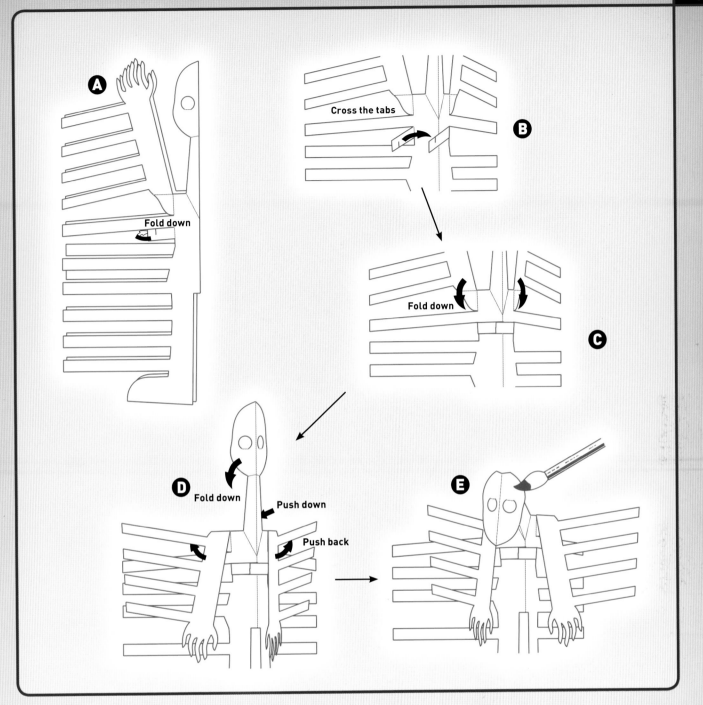

1 Using the Mummy template on pages 114–115, score the folding lines. Then cut along all the solid lines, including the eyes and the tabs for the interlocking joint, as depicted in How to Use This Book on pages 7 – 14. Score and cut out the head bandage template on page 115.

2 Fold the template in half by following the scored centerline. Fold down the tabs for the interlocking joint of the chest. **A**

3 Cross the tabs. **B**

4 Fold down the arms. **C**

5 Push back the arms from the folding lines of the shoulders. Fold down the head while you push down the back of the neck to make the head come forward. **D**

6 Color the face black or any other dark color you like. Draw the eyes. **E**

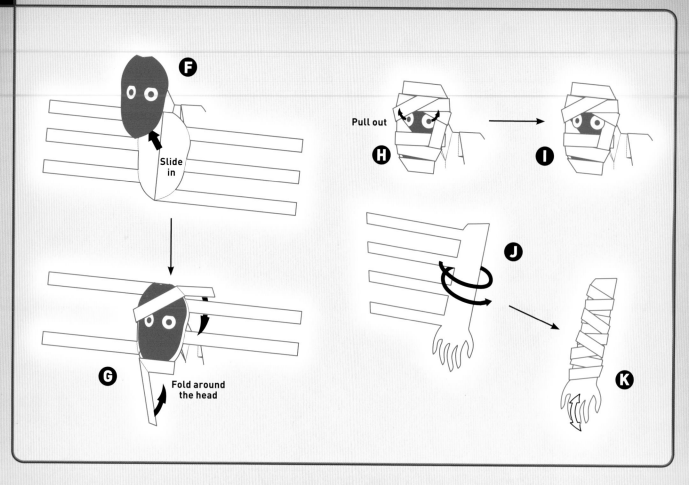

7 Slide the head bandage template underneath the head. **F**

8 Fold the strips over and around the head randomly. How you wrap the head is up to you, but make sure you don't entirely cover the eyes with them. These strips are long so that you can tuck the ends of them under the other strips already in place to secure them. If you find the strips are too long, cut them down to the length you prefer. You can apply a little bit of glue to the ends if you like. Cover the entire head this way by using the project photo for a reference. **G**

9 Pull out the eyes from behind the bandage. You can do this by fishing them out with the tip of the awl you used for scoring. **H** **I**

10 Wrap the entire body of the Mummy the same way as you wrapped the head. Feel free to experiment with wrapping techniques Round the fingers over a dowel. **J** **K**

11 Add color to your Mummy by referencing the project photos.

CURIOUS CREATURES

SPACE ALIENS

DIFFICULTY LEVEL >> **EASY**

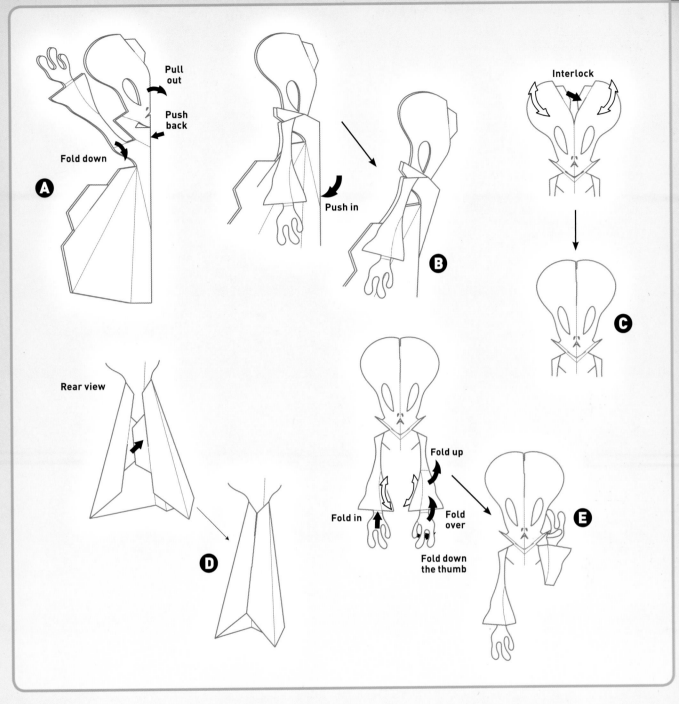

1 Using the Space Alien template on page 115, score the folding lines. Then cut along all the solid lines, including the eyes, the nose, the mouth, the chin, and the tabs for the interlocking joints, as depicted in How to Use This Book on pages 7 – 14.

2 Fold the template in half following the scored centerline. Push back the neck while you pull out the head. Fold down the arms. **A**

3 Push the stomach into the hips. **B**

4 Round the two halves of the head over a dowel. Bring them to the center and cross the tabs of the interlocking joint. **C**

5 Turn the template around. Bring the tabs of the interlocking joint of the lower body together and cross to form the alien's skirt. **D**

6 Work on the arms next. Fold the wrist of the right arm into the sleeve. Fold the wrist of the left arm over the sleeve. Fold down the left thumb. Then fold the left arm up from the elbow joint to create the "we come in peace" pose. **E**

BONUS PROJECTS
Baby Alien and UFO available free at www.larkcrafts.com/bonus

UNICORN

DIFFICULTY LEVEL >> **EASY**

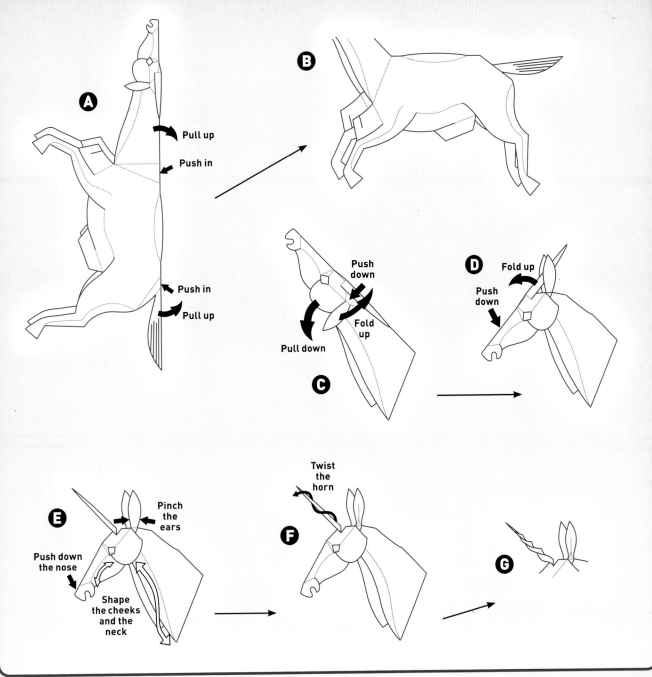

1 Using the Unicorn template on page 113, score the folding lines. Then cut along all the solid lines, including the ears, the eyes, the horn, the tail, and the tabs for the interlocking joints, as depicted in How to Use This Book on pages 7 – 14.

2 Fold the body in half following the scored centerline. Pocket fold the neck into the shoulders and the tail into the hips. **A B**

3 Pull down the head while valley folding its top. Fold up the ears. **C**

4 Push down the lower half of the head below the eyes. Fold up the horn. **D**

5 Add curves to the cheeks by pushing them in following the folding lines. Push down the nose. Push up the cheeks and pinch the ears. Shape the neck. **E**

6 Twist the horn with your fingers to turn it into a spiral. **F G**

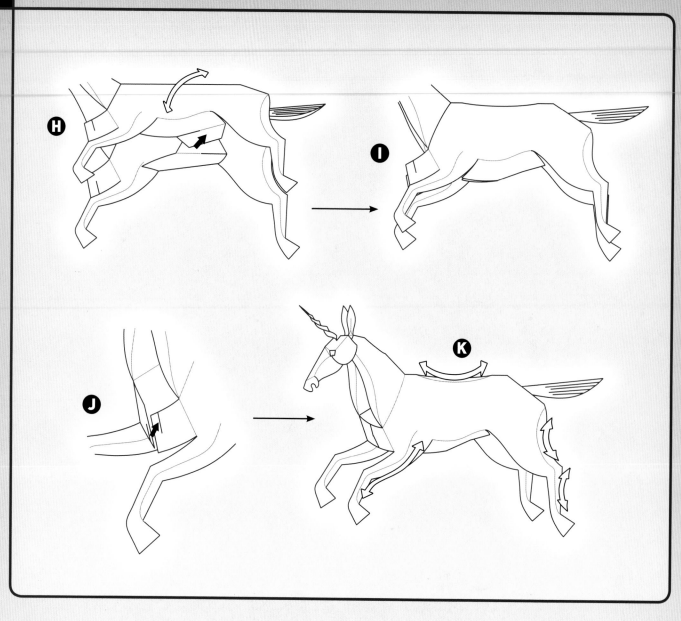

7 Round the body. Interlock the stomach joint by crossing the tabs. **H** **I**

8 Interlock the chest joint by crossing the tabs. **J**

9 Shape the back and the front and hind legs by following the folding lines. **K**

10 Add color to your Unicorn by referencing the project photos.

BIGFOOT

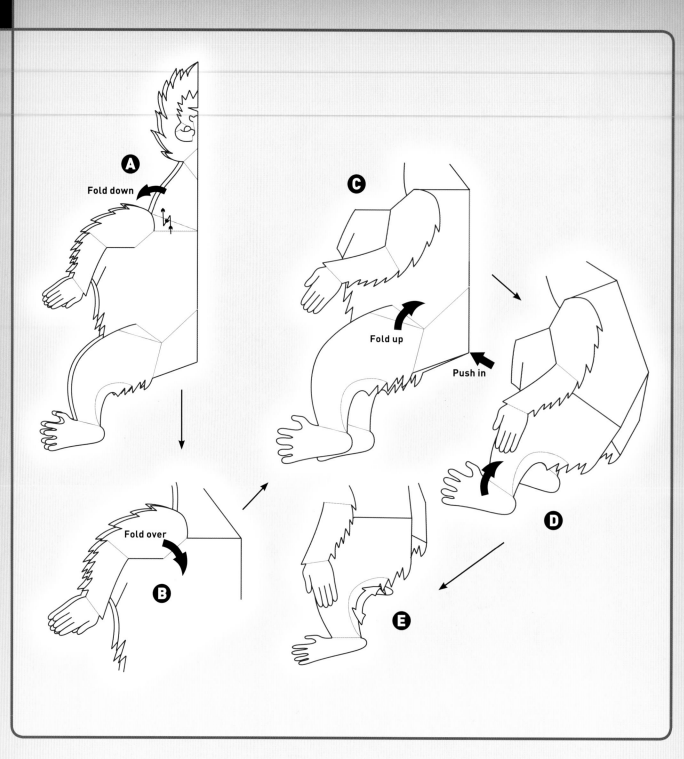

1 Using the Big Foot template on page 116, score the folding lines. Then cut along all the solid lines, including the eyes, the nose, the mouth, and the tabs for the interlocking joint, as depicted in How to Use This Book on pages 7 – 14.

2 Fold the body in half following the scored centerline. Fold down the neck into the shoulders. Ⓐ

3 Fold over the arms to back. Ⓑ

4 Fold up the legs on the sides of the hips while you push in the bottom of the hips. Ⓒ

5 Fold up the feet to the outsides. Ⓓ

6 Shape the back of the legs following the scored lines. Ⓔ

7 Pull down the head while you valley fold its top. Unfold the head. Ⓕ

8 Add more dimensionality to the face by squeezing in the cheeks and pushing up the eyes toward the forehead. Ⓖ

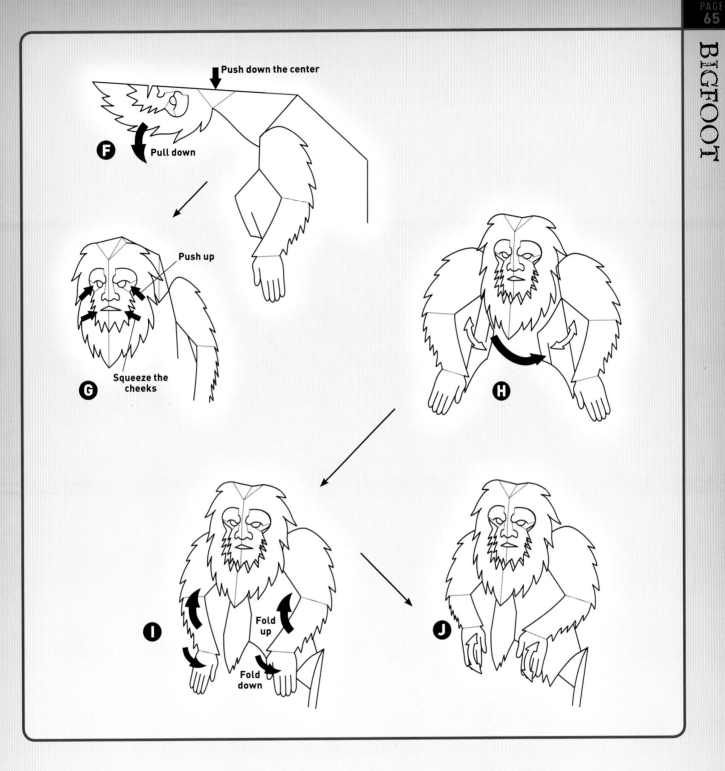

Push down the center

Pull down

F

Push up

Squeeze the cheeks

G

H

I

Fold up

Fold down

J

9 Round the two halves of the chest over a dowel. Bring them to the center and cross the tabs for the interlocking joint. **H**

10 Fold up the forearms, then fold down the hands. **I**

11 Roll the hands over a dowel. **J**

12 Adjust the angle of the feet so Big Foot can stand securely.

13 Add color to your Big Foot by referencing the project photos.

VARIATION

Make this project with a sheet of white card stock, and you'll have an Abominable Snowman instead!

MINOTAUR

DIFFICULTY LEVEL >> **INTERMEDIATE**

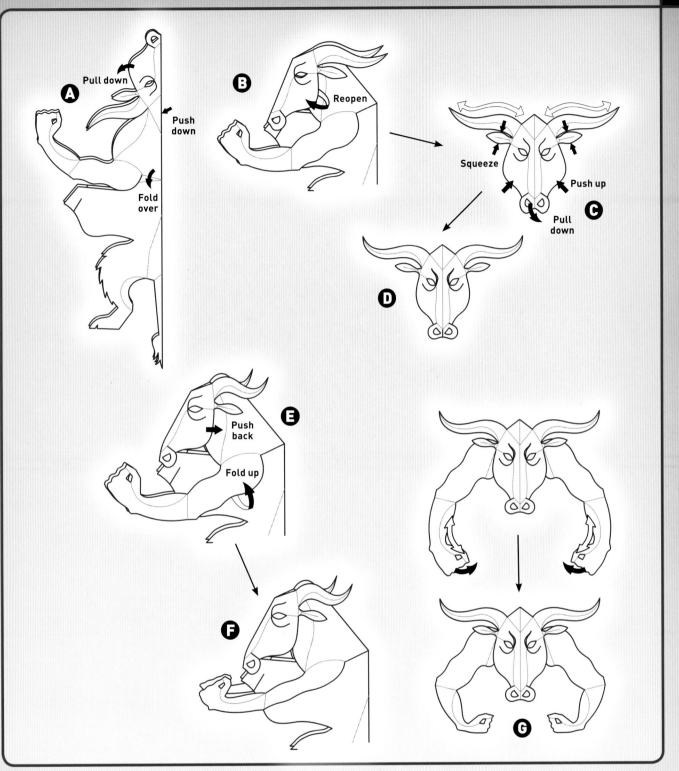

1 Using the Minotaur template on page 117, score the folding lines. Then cut along all the solid lines, including the eyes, the nose, the hands, and the tabs for an interlocking joint, as depicted in How to Use This Book on pages 7 – 14.

2 Fold the body in half following the scored centerline. Then fold the shoulders over the chest. Pull down the head while valley folding the top of the head. **A**

3 Unfold the head and open it up. **B**

4 Shape the horns following the scored centerlines. Pinch and squeeze the ears. Push up the cheeks. Pull down the nose. **C D**

5 Push in the front sides of the neck from the folding lines. Fold up the arms from the shoulder lines to the sides of the body. **E F**

6 Shape the forearms following the scored lines. Bring both forearms closer to the center of the chest. **G**

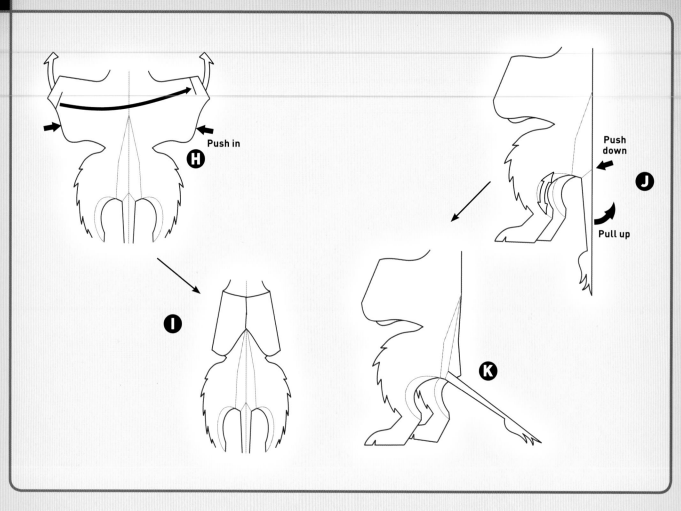

Push in

Push down

Pull up

H

I

J

K

7 Roll the two halves of the chest over a dowel. Bring them to the front and interlock the chest joint by crossing the tabs. **H** **I**

8 Raise the tail while pushing its base into the hips. Shape the legs. **J** **K**

9 Adjust the angles of the legs and the tail so that your Minotaur will stand securely.

10 Add color to your Minotaur by referencing the project photos.

11 You can find the template for your Minotaur's axe on page 117. Cut it out and color it however you like. Make the Minotaur hold the axe by running the handle through the opening of his hand.

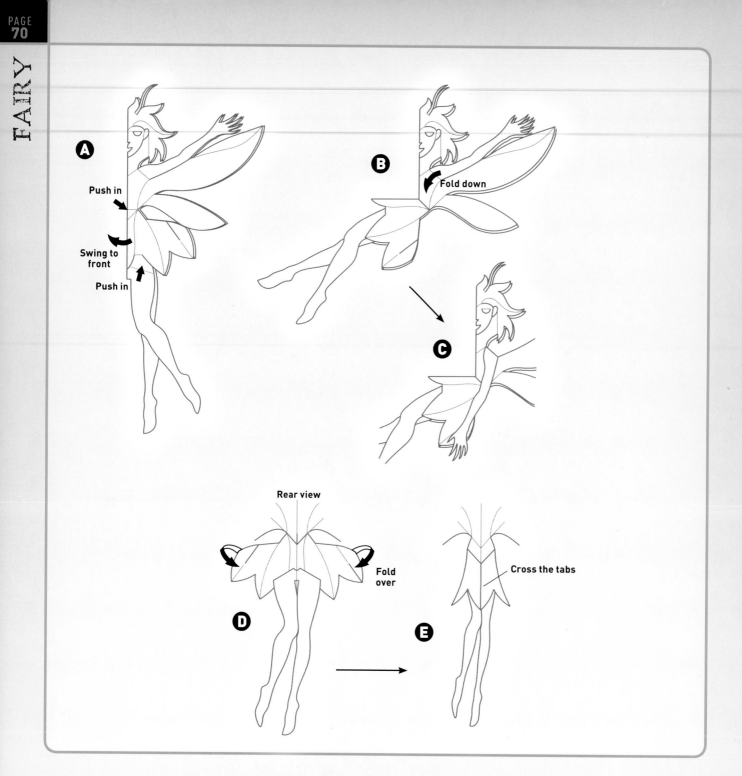

1 Using the Fairy template on page 118, score the folding lines. Then cut along all the solid lines, including the eyes, the nose, the mouth, the antennae, the front flap of the skirt, and the tabs for the interlocking joint, as depicted in How to Use This Book on pages 7 – 14.

2 Fold the template in half by following the scored centerline. Pocket fold the upper body into the lower body by pushing in the triangle shape of the stomach while you swing the hips to the front (don't push in the triangle shape if you want your fairy to fly horizontally. See step 12). Fold and push in the legs under the skirt. **A**

3 Fold down the arms from the shoulders. **B** **C**

4 Turn the template over to the back. Fold over both tabs for the interlocking joint to the back. **D**

5 Bring the tabs to the center and cross the tabs to create the skirt. **E**

F

Fold down

Pull up

Squeeze

G

Pull back

Push in

H

I

Fold out

No folding
for flying
fairy

J

6 Work on the head next. Pull up the eyelids. Fold down the antennae. Pinch and squeeze the cheeks. **F**

7 Push in the center of the throat while you slightly pull back the top of the head. Use the vertical folding lines on the sides of the face as a guide for shaping. The face of the Fairy will come forward naturally. **G**

8 Shape the hair. Use a dowel to create smooth wavy curves. **H**

9 Add curves to the bases of the large wings. Shape the front edges of them following the scored folding lines. Fold the small wings out to the sides. **I**

10 The balancing center of the Fairy's body is marked with an X on the template. Run a thread through this mark to hang your Fairy.

11 Add color to your Fairy by referencing the project photos.

12 You have another option for posing your Fairy: If you don't pocket fold the triangle shape of her stomach (in step 2), you can make her fly horizontally. **J**

CYCLOPS

DIFFICULTY LEVEL >> **INTERMEDIATE**

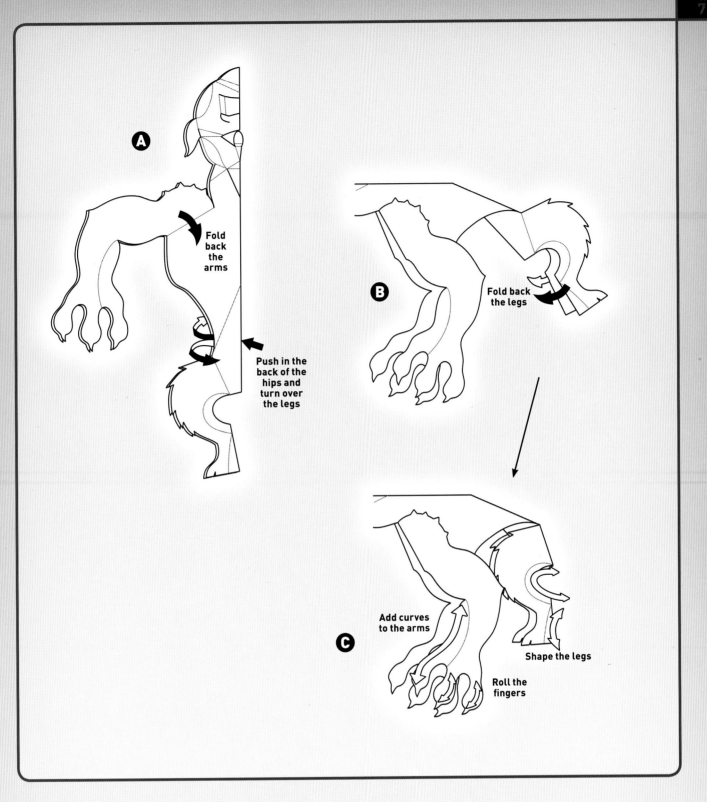

A

Fold back the arms

Push in the back of the hips and turn over the legs

B

Fold back the legs

C

Add curves to the arms

Shape the legs

Roll the fingers

1 Using the Cyclops template on page 119, score the folding lines. Then cut along all the solid lines, including the horn, the eye, the nose, and the mouth, as depicted in How to Use This Book on pages 7 – 14.

2 Fold the body in half following the scored centerline. Leave the eye unfolded. Push down the back of the hips and turn over the legs. Fold back the arms over the shoulders. **A**

3 Fold back the legs to the front. **B**

4 Fold the forearms along the scored lines and add curves to them. Roll the fingers over a dowel. Shape the legs. **C**

GARGOYLE

1 Using the Gargoyle template on page 120, score the folding lines. Then cut along all the solid lines, including the eyes, the nose, and the mouth, as depicted in How to Use This Book on pages 7 – 14.

2 Fold the template in half by following the scored centerline. Fold up the wings while you push down the back of the Gargoyle. Pull down the arms and pull up the legs. **A**

3 Pull up the head while you push down the back of the neck and pocket fold it into the shoulders. **B**

4 Push down and valley fold the top of the head while you pull down the head toward the legs. **C D**

5 Pinch and squeeze the ears. Push in the bases of the ears behind the forehead. Push up the mouth into the cheeks. **E**

6 Fold down the horns slightly. Push up the cheeks toward the eyes. Shape the cheeks following the scored folding lines. **F**

7 Unfold the head a bit. **G**

8 Fold out the upper arms, fold in the forearms, and fold out the hands. **H**

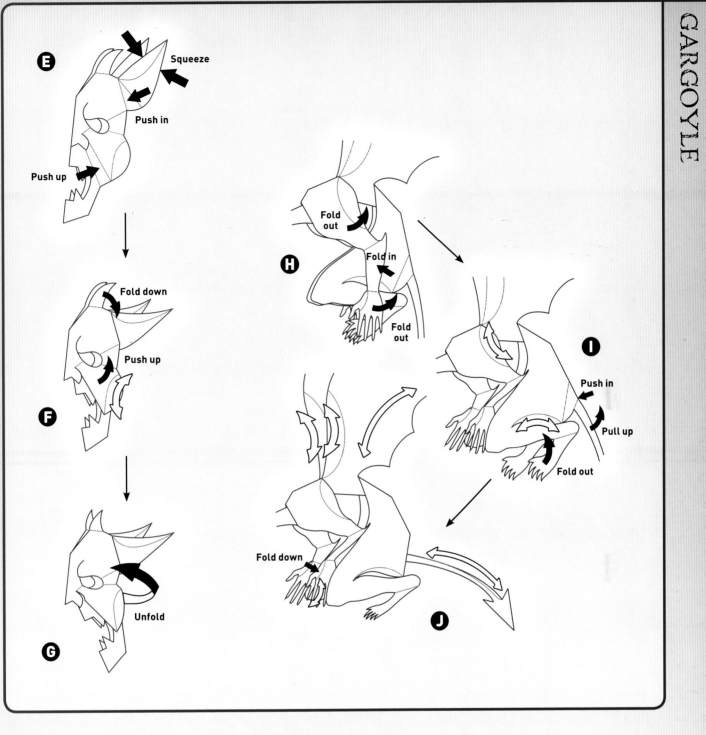

E Squeeze
Push in
Push up

Fold down
Push up
F

Unfold
G

H Fold out
Fold in
Fold out

I Push in
Pull up
Fold out

Fold down
J

9 Fold the feet out to the sides. Shape the thighs. Push the base of the tail into the hips while you pull up the tail. **I**

10 Fold down the thumbs. Roll the fingers over a dowel. Shape the wings and the tail following the scored folding lines. **J**

11 Adjust the angles of the legs, hands, and tail so that your Gargoyle will sit comfortably.

12 Add color to your Gargoyle by referencing the project photos.

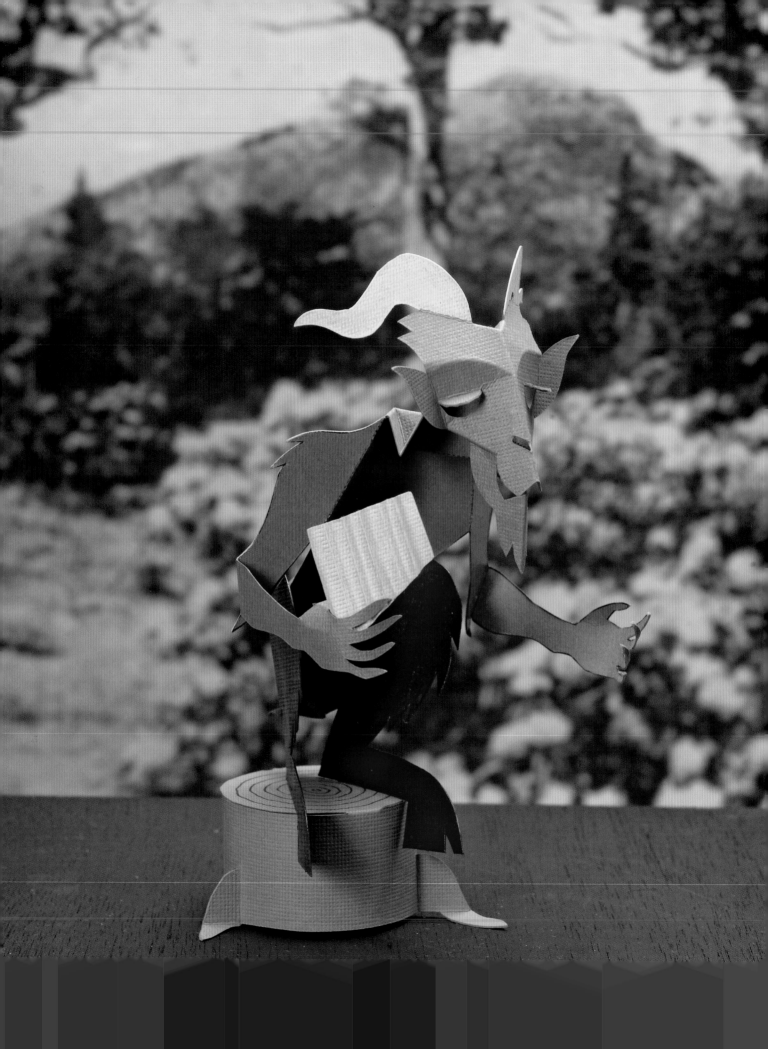

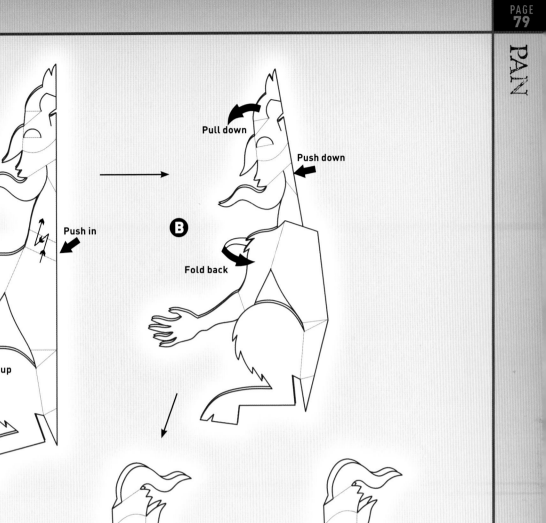

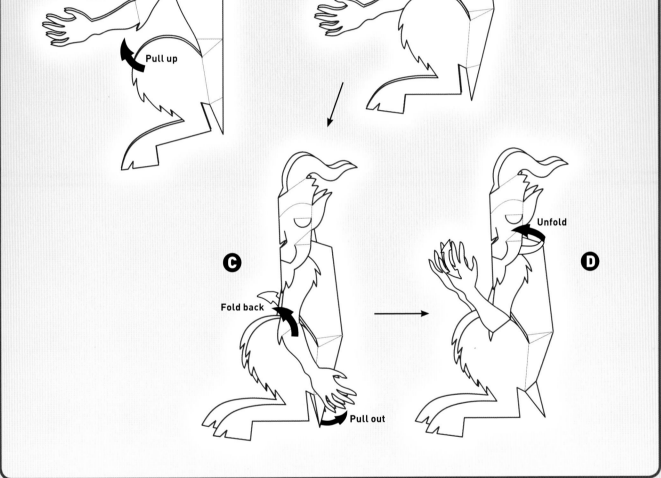

1 Using the Pan template on page 121, score the folding lines. Then cut along all the solid lines, including the eyes, nose, and mouth, as depicted in How to Use This Book on pages 7 – 14.

2 Fold the template in half following the scored centerline. Push the neck into the shoulders. Pull up the legs to the front. **A**

3 Pull down the head while you valley fold the top. Fold back the arms. **B**

4 Fold back the forearms. Pull out the tail. **C**

5 Unfold the face. Roll the fingers over a dowel. **D**

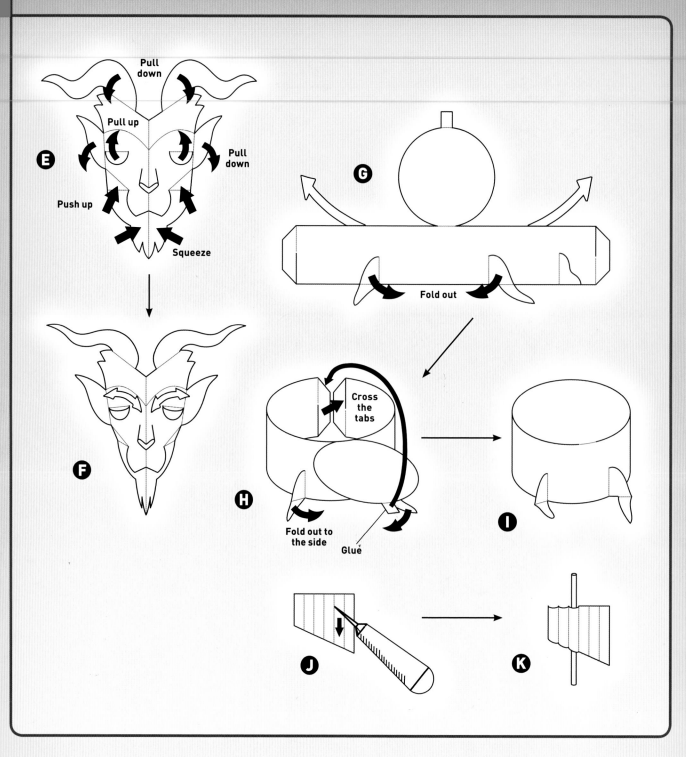

6 Pull up the eyelids. Pull down the horns and the ears slightly. Push up the cheeks while you pinch and squeeze the chin. **E**

7 Add a curve to the area under the eyebrows. **F**

8 Score and cut out the tree stump and flute templates on page 121.

9 Roll the side of the tree stump over a dowel to round it. Fold out the roots to the side. **G**

10 Cross the tabs for the interlocking joint in the back. Fold down the lid on top and glue the small tab to the inside of the joint you just worked on. Fold out the tips of the roots so that the tree stump stands securely. **H** **I**

11 Score the dashed lines of the flute. **J**

12 Roll each section of the flute over a thin dowel to round them. **K**

13 Add color to your Pan by referencing the project photos. Make him sit on the tree stump and hold the flute in his hands.

Merak

PERSEUS

THE GREAT BEAR

Algol

OVER-HEAD

Capella

E CRAB

THE CHARIOTEER

Castor

Pollux

The Pl

The Hyades

Aldeba

ORION

Procyon

E

ENT

R

THE

PEGASUS

PAGE
81

DIFFICULTY LEVEL >> INTERMEDIATE

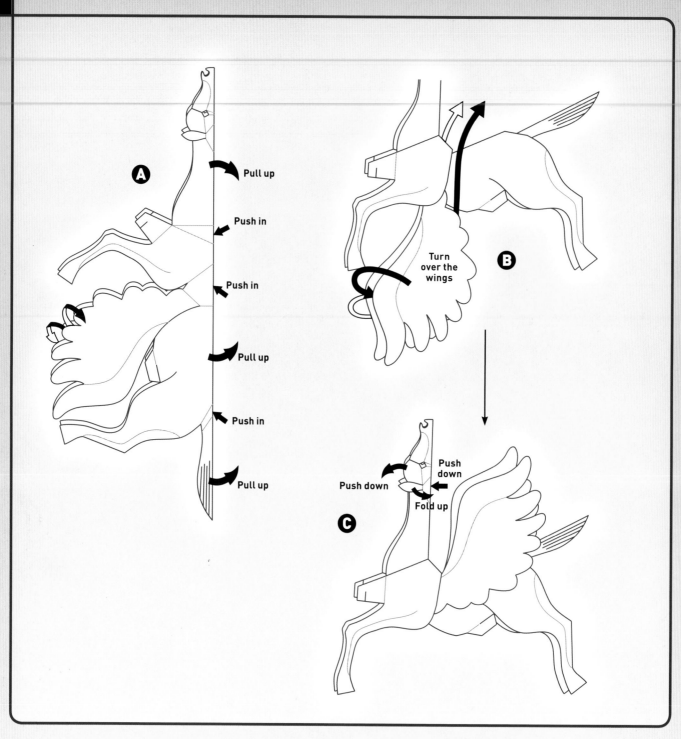

A Pull up

Push in

Push in

Pull up

Push in

Pull up

B Turn over the wings

C Push down

Push down

Fold up

1 Using the Pegasus template on page 122, score the folding lines. Then cut along all the solid lines, including the ears, the eyes, the tail, and the tabs for the interlocking joints, as depicted in How to Use This Book on pages 7 – 14.

2 Fold the body in half following the scored centerline. Pocket fold the neck into the shoulders, the lower body into the upper body, and the tail into the hips. When the lower body is pocket folded into the upper body, the wings will be naturally reversed. **A**

3 Raise the wings to the sides of the body by turning them over from the folding lines at their base. **B**

4 Pull down the head while valley folding the center of its top. Fold up the ears. **C**

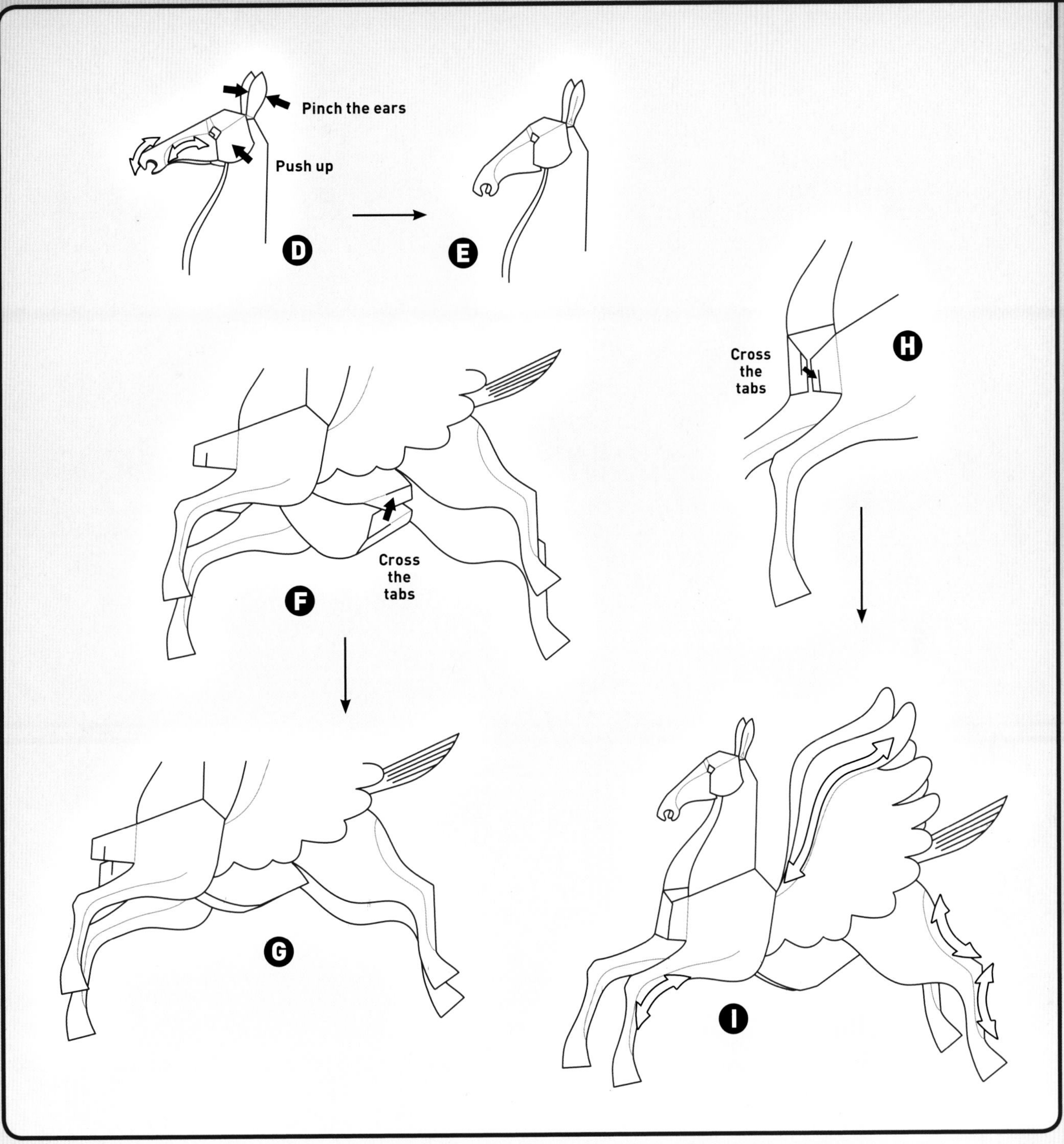

Pinch the ears

Push up

D

E

Cross
the
tabs

H

Cross
the
tabs

F

G

I

5 Add curves to the cheeks by pushing them in following the folding lines. Round the nose. Push up the cheeks and pinch the ears. **D** **E**

6 Interlock the stomach joint by crossing the tabs. **F** **G**

7 Interlock the chest joint by crossing the tabs. **H**

8 Shape the wings and the front and hind legs by following the folding lines. **I**

9 Add color to your Pegasus by referencing the project photos.

QUASIMODO

DIFFICULTY LEVEL ≫ INTERMEDIATE

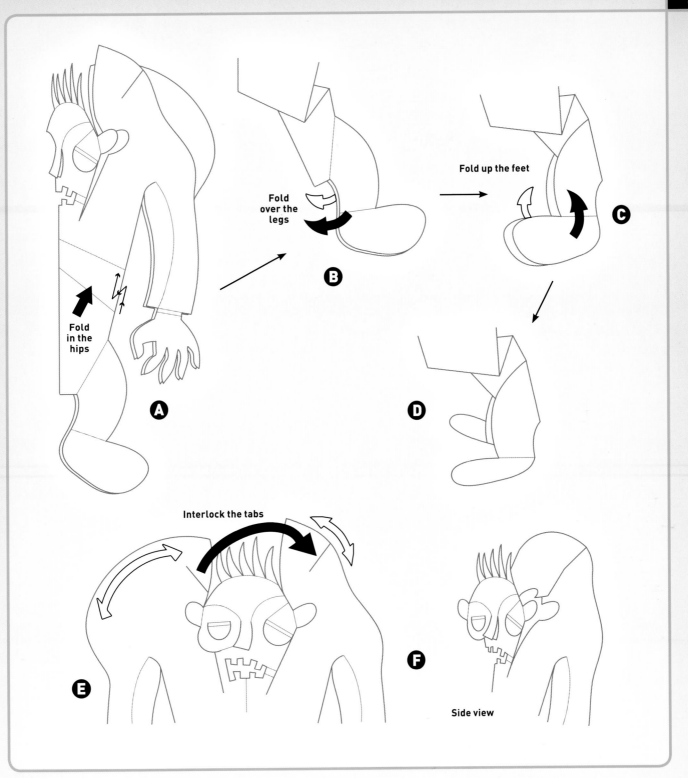

Fold
over the
legs

Fold up the feet

B

C

Fold
in the
hips

A

D

Interlock the tabs

E

F

Side view

1 Using the Quasimodo template on page 123, score the folding lines. Then cut along all the solid lines, including the eyes, the hair, the nose, the mouth, and the tabs for the interlocking joint, as depicted in How to Use This Book on pages 7 – 14.

2 Fold the body in half following the scored centerline. Leave the head unfolded. Fold in the hips under the upper body. **A**

3 Fold over the legs to the front. **B**

4 Fold up the feet to the sides. **C D**

5 Roll the two halves of the back over a dowel, bring them to the center, and interlock the tabs behind the head. **E F**

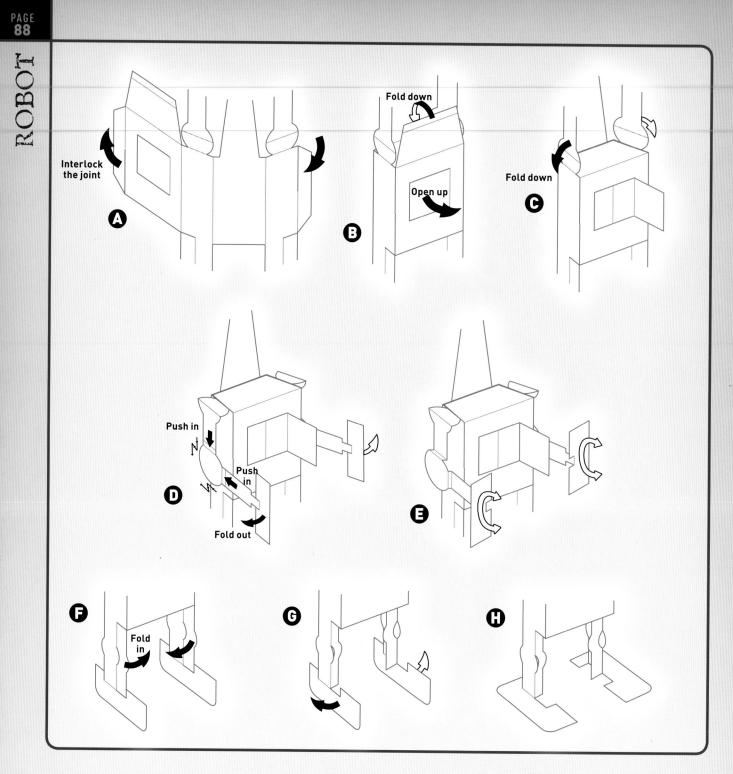

1 Using the Robot template on page 124, score the folding lines. Then cut along all the solid lines, including the eyes, ears, mouth, the plate in the stomach, and the tabs for the interlocking joint, as depicted in How to Use This Book on pages 7 – 14.

2 Fold the body, cross the tabs for the interlocking joint, and fold the body into a box shape. **A**

3 Fold down the top of the body. Open up the door in the chest. **B**

4 Fold down both arms by following the folding lines of the shoulders. **C**

5 Push the upper arm and the forearm into the elbow joint. Fold out the hands. **D**

6 Roll the hands over a dowel to round them. **E**

7 Fold the legs in half by following the scored centerlines. **F**

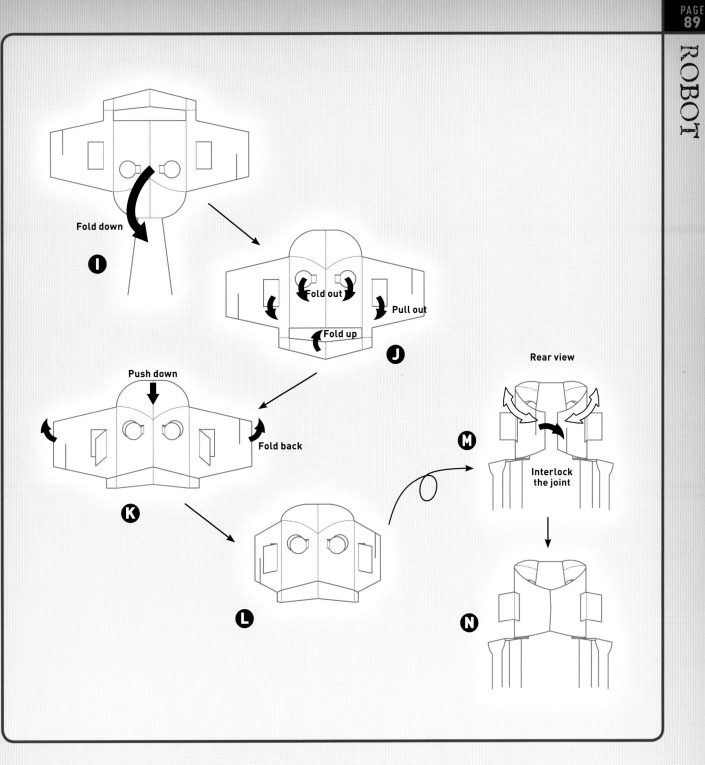

Fold down

I

Fold out

Pull out

Fold up

J

Push down

Fold back

K

L

Rear view

Interlock
the joint

M

N

8 Fold the feet out next so that your Robot will stand comfortably. **G** **H**

9 Fold the head down over the neck. **I**

10 Fold out the eyes. Pull out the ears. Fold up the lower jaw over the mouth. **J**

11 Push down the center of the head. Fold back the two sides of the head. **K** **L**

12 Roll the sides of the head. Bring them to the center and interlock the joint in the back. **M** **N**

13 Add color to your Robot and draw the eyes and the mechanism inside the stomach by referencing the project photos.

CREATURE FROM THE BLACK LAGOON

DIFFICULTY LEVEL ≫ ADVANCED

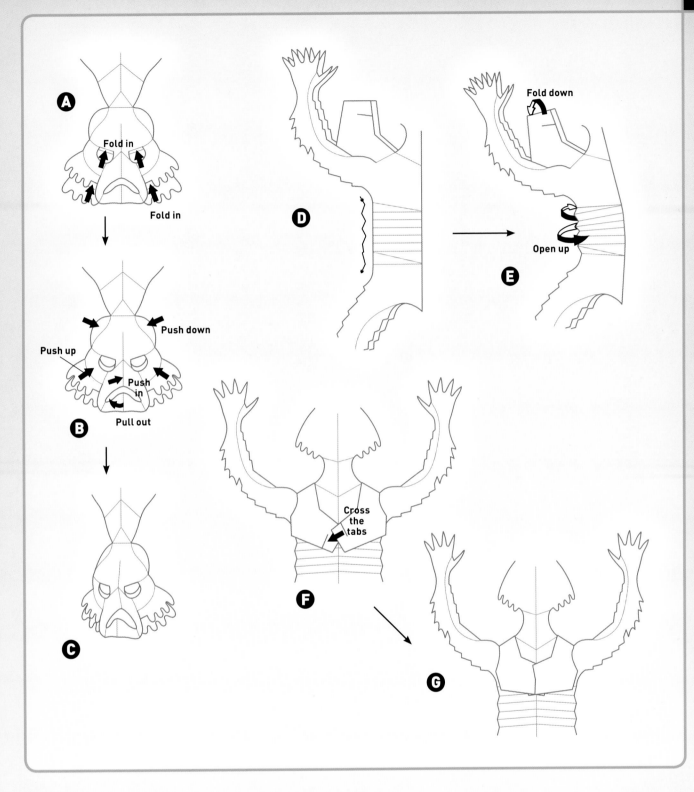

1 Using the Creature from the Black Lagoon template on page 125, score the folding lines. Then cut along all the solid lines, including the eyes, the mouth, the gills, and the tabs for the interlocking joint, as depicted in How to Use This Book on pages 7 – 14.

2 Fold in the eyes and the gills under the cheeks. Ⓐ

3 Push in the nose area while pulling out the chin. Push up the cheeks and push down the sides of the head. Ⓑ Ⓒ

4 Fold the body in half by following the scored centerline. Fold the

stomach in a series of peak folds and valley folds so that it looks like a bellows. Open up the body a little and fold down the chest plates. Ⓓ Ⓔ

5 Bring the two halves of the chest closer and cross the tabs to connect them. Ⓕ Ⓖ

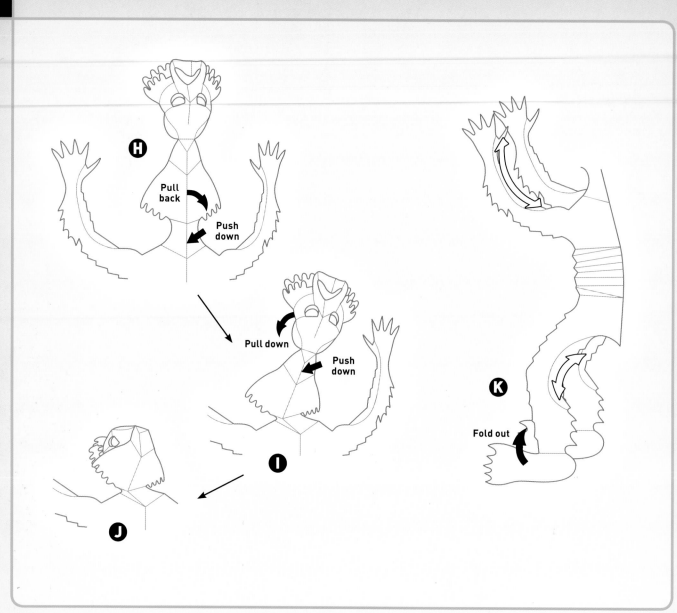

6 Turn the template over. Push down the neck into the shoulders. Pull back the head. **H**

7 Push down and valley fold the top of the head while you pull the face down to the front. **I** **J**

8 Fold the feet out to the sides. Shape the arms and the legs following the scored folding lines in them. Adjust the angles of the feet, legs, and stomach so that the Creature can stand on his feet. **K**

9 Add color to your Creature by referencing the project photos.

GRYPHON

DIFFICULTY LEVEL >> **ADVANCED**

GRYPHON

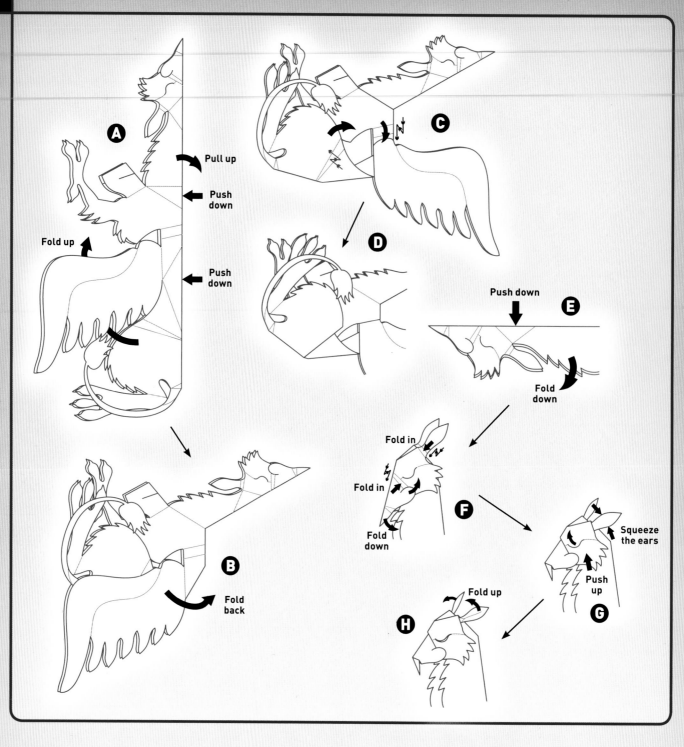

Pull up

Push down

Fold up

Push down

A

B

Fold back

C

D

Push down

E

Fold down

Fold in

Fold in

F

Fold down

Squeeze the ears

Push up

G

Fold up

H

1 Using the Gryphon template on page 126, score the folding lines. Then cut along all the solid lines, including the eyes, the beak, and the tabs for the interlocking joint, as depicted in How to Use This Book on pages 7 – 14.

2 Fold the template in half by following the scored centerline. Push down the back of the neck and pocket fold the neck into the

shoulders. Push down the center of the Gryphon's back and fold up the lower half of the body toward the chest. **A**

3 Fold back the wings. **B**

4 Pocket fold the wings into the shoulders. The shoulders should cover the bases of the wings. Fold the hind legs over the front legs. **C D**

5 Fold down the neck behind the head while you valley fold the top of the head. **E**

6 Fold the bases of the ears into the head. Fold the top of the beak under the eyes while making the sides of the beak partially cover the cheeks. Fold down the tip of the beak. **F**

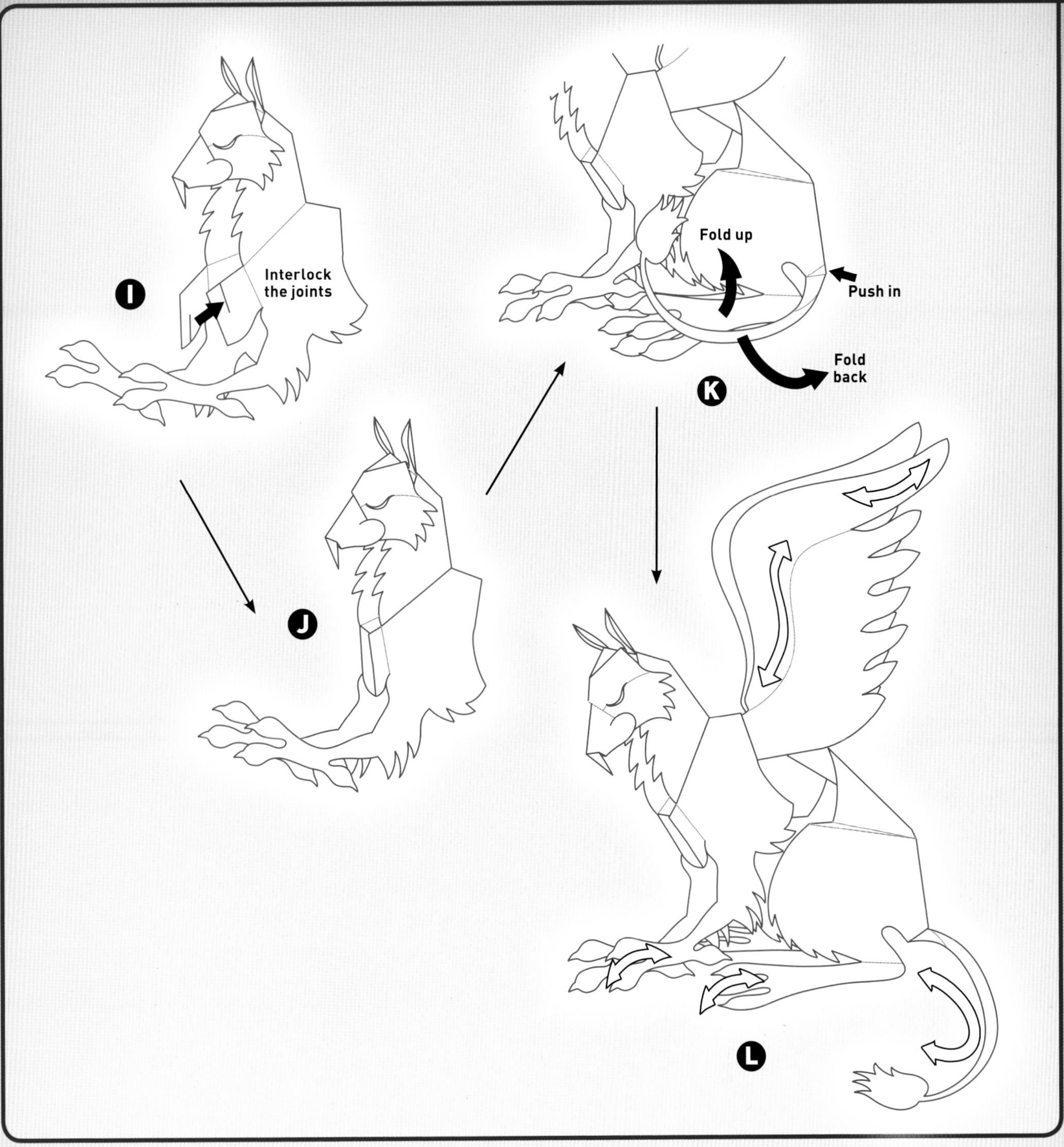

Interlock
the joints

I

J

Fold up

Push in

Fold
back

K

L

7 Pinch and squeeze the ears to shape them. Push up the cheeks. Roll up the eyelids to open up the eyes. **G**

8 Fold up the ears toward the forehead. **H**

9 Pull the tabs together and interlock the chest joint. **I** **J**

10 Push the base of the tail into the hips and fold back the entire tail. Fold up the feet to the sides of the body. **K**

11 Roll the tail over a dowel to add a curve to it. Roll all four feet over a dowel. Following the scored folding lines, shape the wings. **L**

12 Add color to your Gryphon by referencing the project photos.

A Push in · Push down · Fold up

B Push down · Fold up · Pull down · Fold over · Fold over

C

D Pull up · Cross the tabs

E Push down

F

1 Using the Dragon template on page 127, score the folding lines. Then cut along all the solid lines, including the eyes, the nose, the mouth, and the tabs for the interlocking joints, as depicted in How to Use This Book on pages 7 – 14.

2 Fold the template in half by following the scored centerline.

Push in the bottom of the neck while pushing in the shoulders. Fold up the wings to the back. **A**

3 Fold up the horns. Pull down the head while you push down and valley fold the top of the head. Fold the shoulders over the bases of the wings. Fold up the thighs over the hips. **B**

4 Shape the wings by rolling them over a dowel. **C**

5 Pull up the eyelids. Interlock the joint of the lower jaw by crossing the tabs. **D**

6 Push down the nose and fold down the fangs. Shape the neckline. **E** **F**

DRAGON

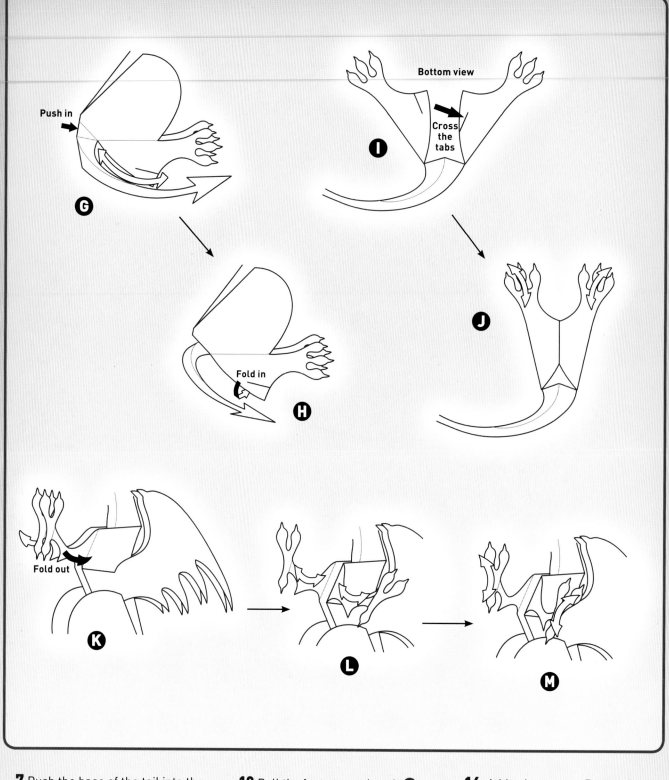

Push in

G

Bottom view

Cross
the
tabs

I

Fold in

H

J

Fold out

K

L

M

7 Push the base of the tail into the hips. Shape the tail by following its scored line. **G**

8 Fold in the tabs of the legs under the hips. **H**

9 Cross the tabs and interlock the joint of the legs. **I**

10 Roll the feet over a dowel. **J**

11 Fold out the arms to the sides. **K**

12 Roll the arms over a dowel. **L**

13 Roll the fingers over a dowel. **M**

14 Add color to your Dragon by referencing the project photos.

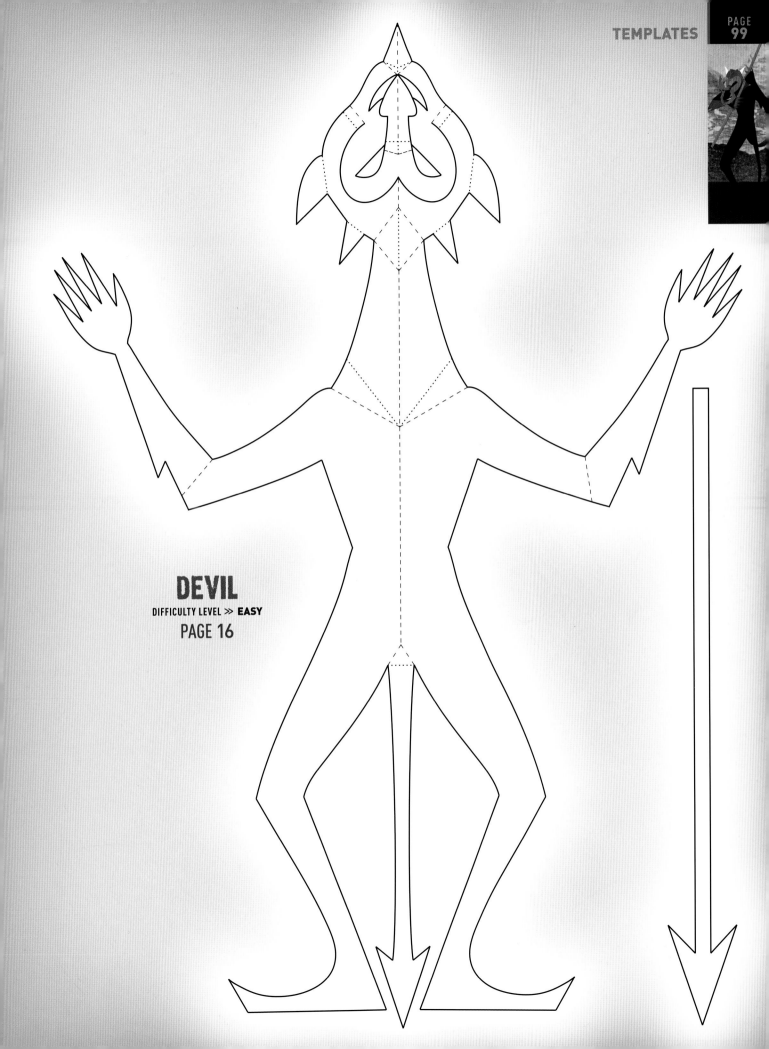

DEVIL
DIFFICULTY LEVEL >> **EASY**
PAGE 16

LOCH NESS
MONSTER
DIFFICULTY LEVEL ≫ EASY
PAGE 20

SWAMP THING
DIFFICULTY LEVEL >> INTERMEDIATE
PAGE 36

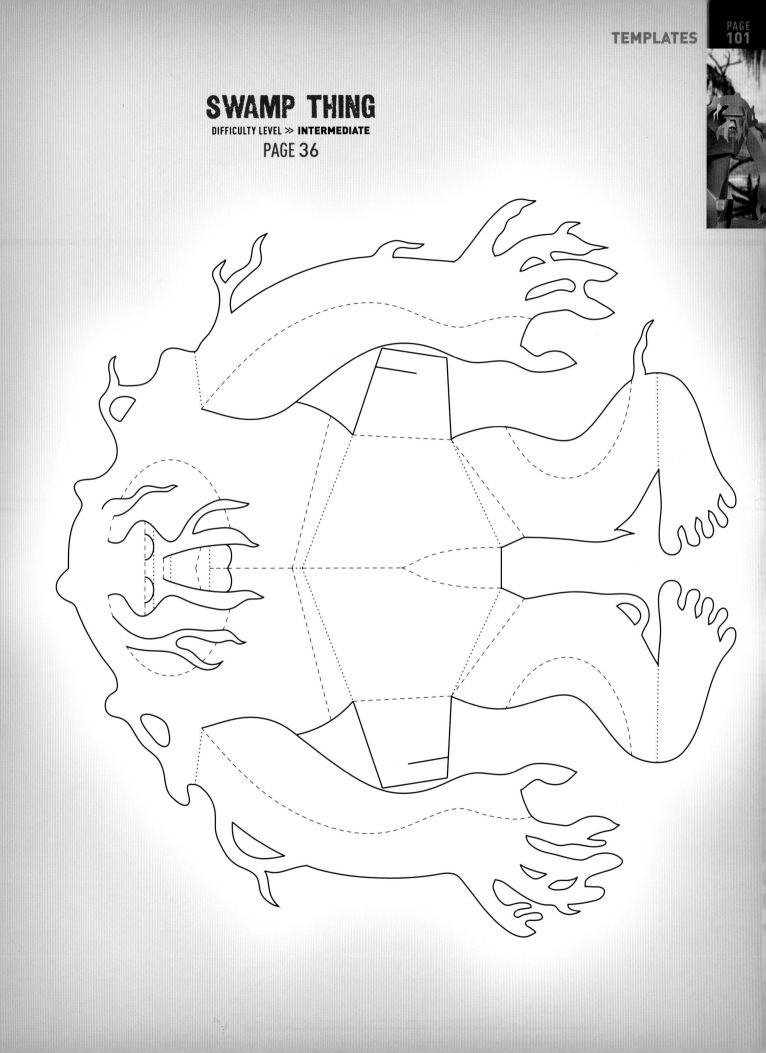

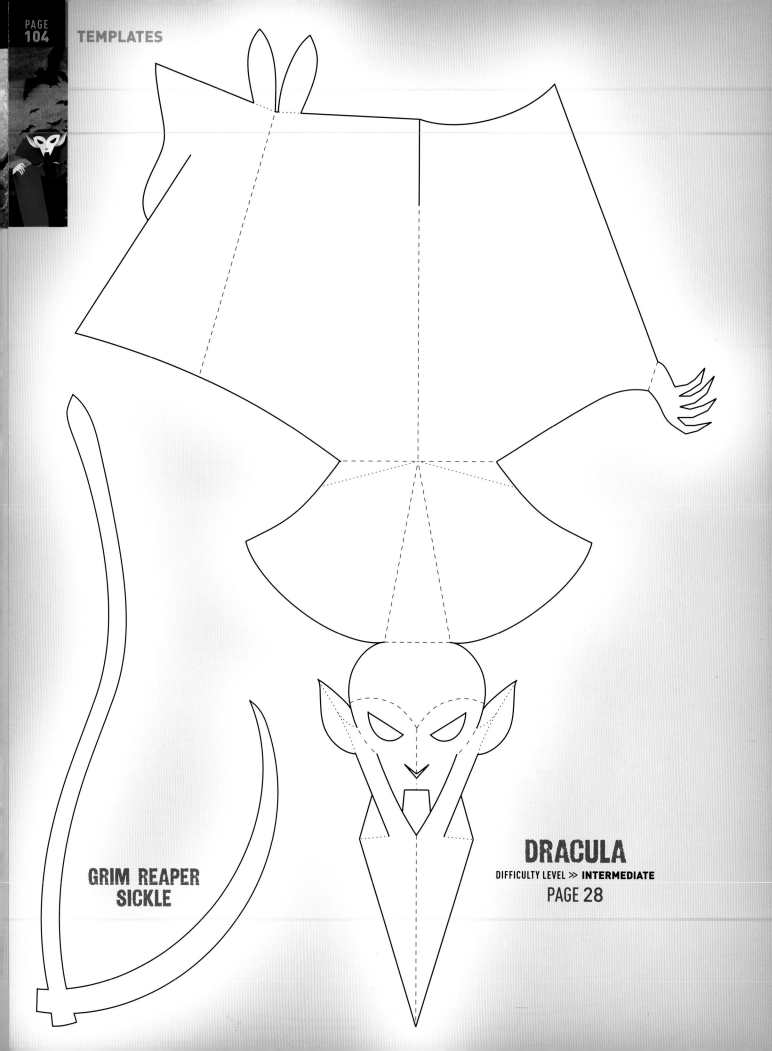

GRIM REAPER
SICKLE

DRACULA
DIFFICULTY LEVEL » INTERMEDIATE
PAGE 28

GRIM REAPER
DIFFICULTY LEVEL ≫ **INTERMEDIATE**
PAGE 30

WOLFMAN
DIFFICULTY LEVEL >> INTERMEDIATE
PAGE 41

ZOMBIE
DIFFICULTY LEVEL >> INTERMEDIATE
PAGE 44

KRAKEN
DIFFICULTY LEVEL >> **ADVANCED**
PAGE 46

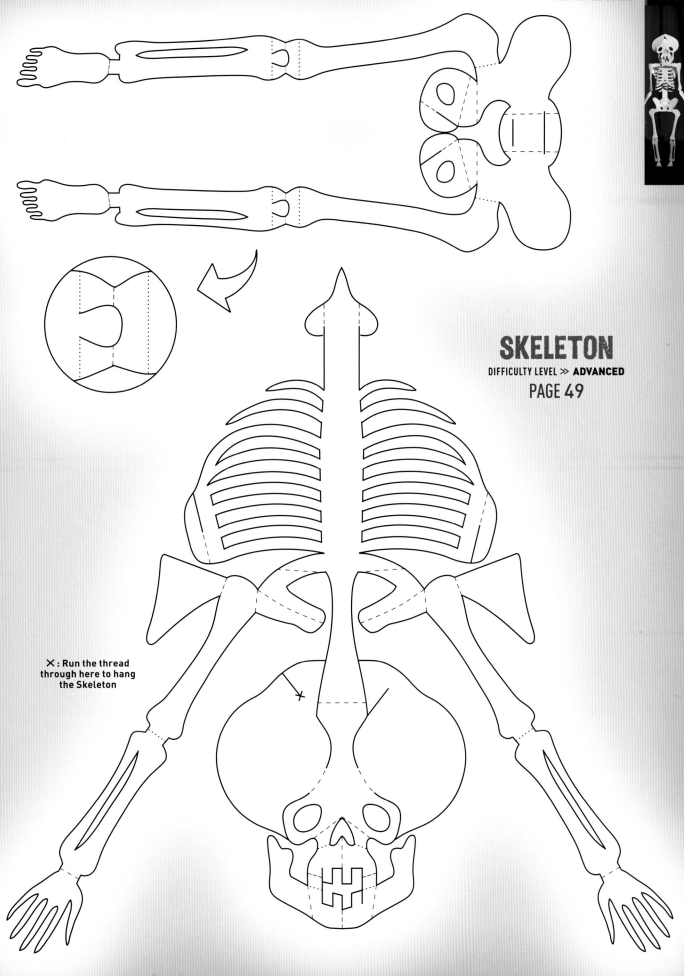

SKELETON
DIFFICULTY LEVEL >> **ADVANCED**
PAGE 49

✕ : Run the thread
through here to hang
the Skeleton

MEDUSA

DIFFICULTY LEVEL ≫ **ADVANCED**

PAGE 52

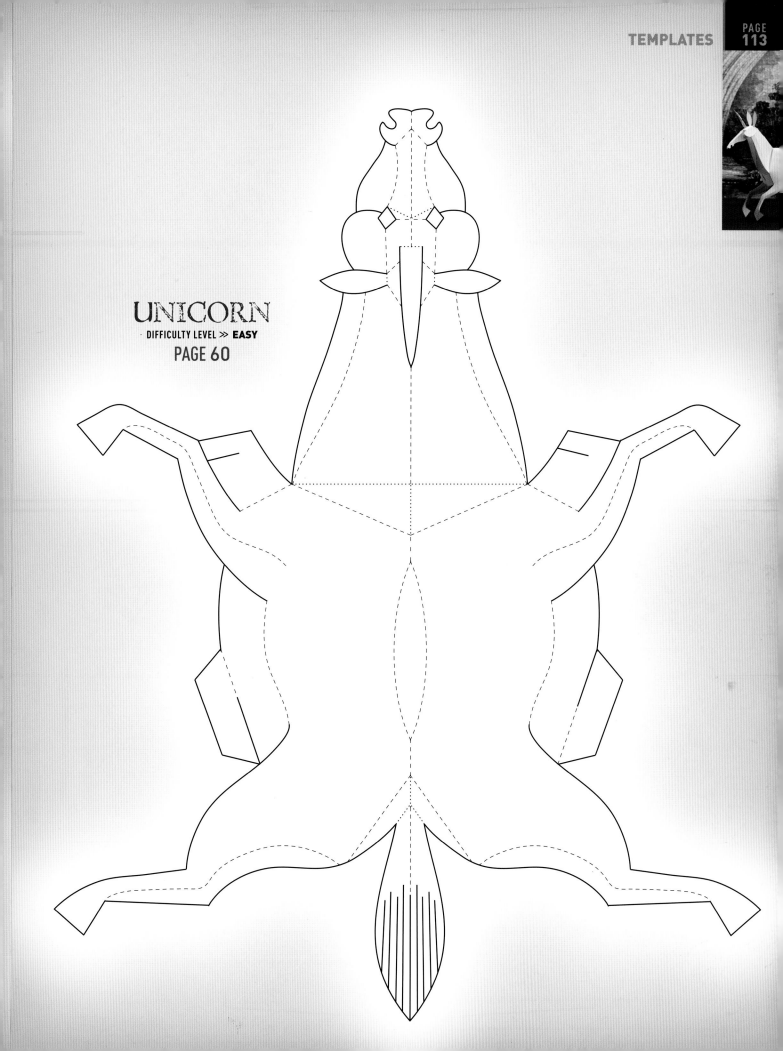

UNICORN

· DIFFICULTY LEVEL ≫ **EASY**

PAGE 60

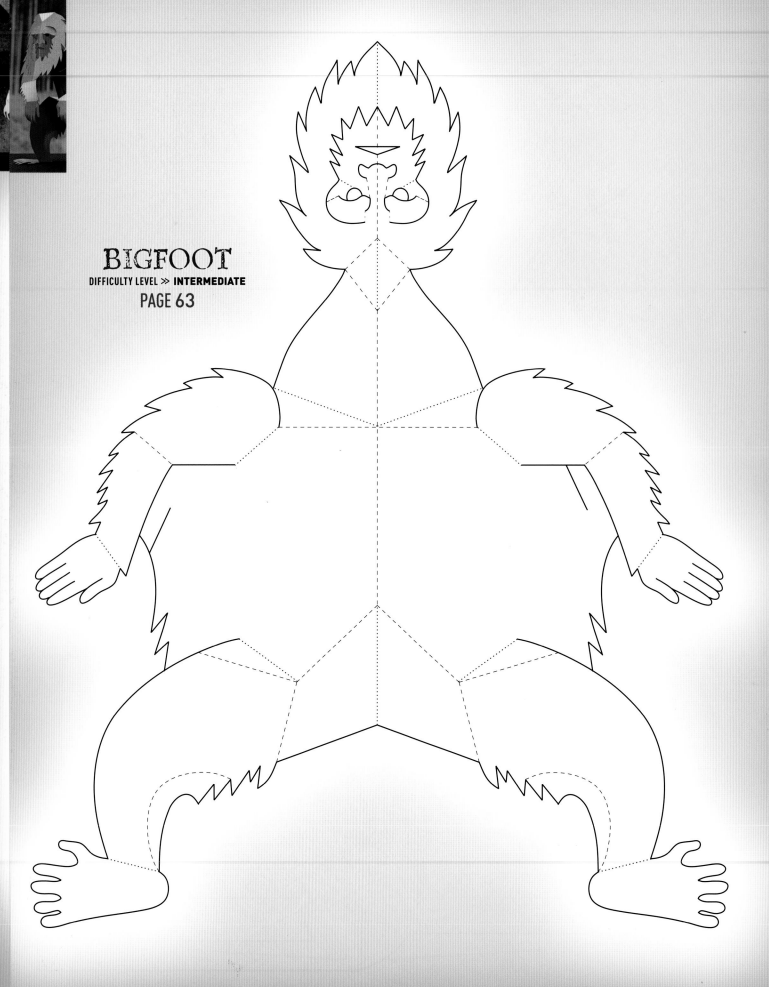

BIGFOOT
DIFFICULTY LEVEL » INTERMEDIATE
PAGE 63

MINOTAUR

DIFFICULTY LEVEL >> INTERMEDIATE

PAGE 66

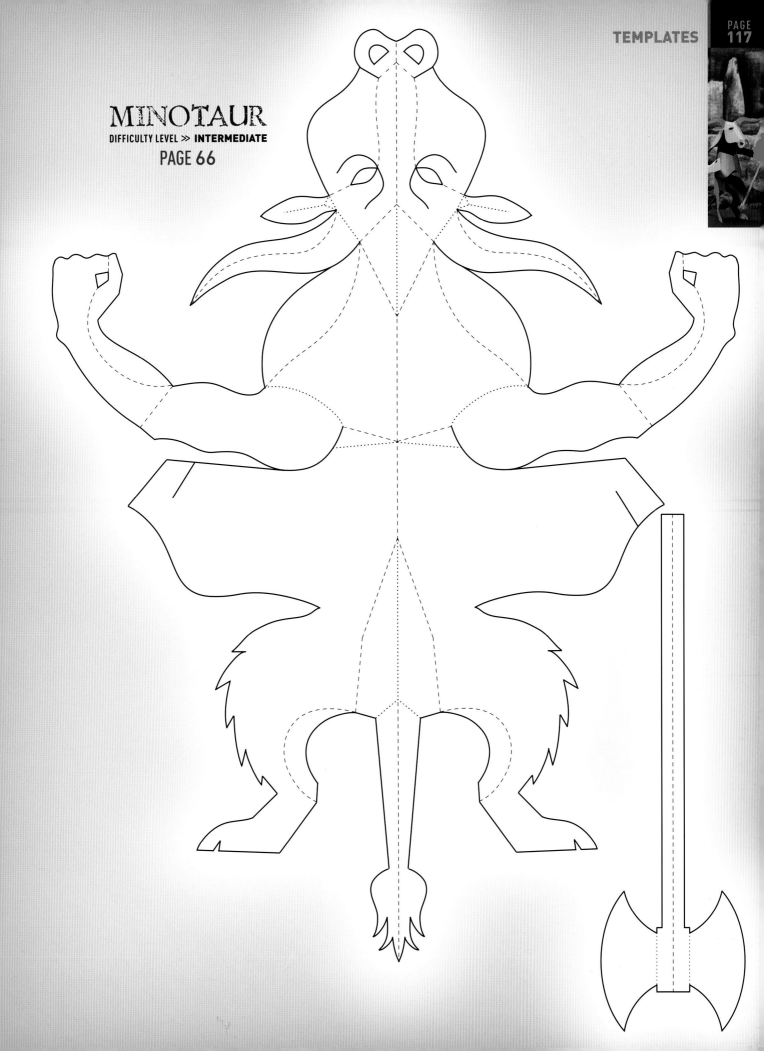

✕ : Run the thread
through here to hang
the Fairy

FAIRY
DIFFICULTY LEVEL ≫ **INTERMEDIATE**
PAGE 69

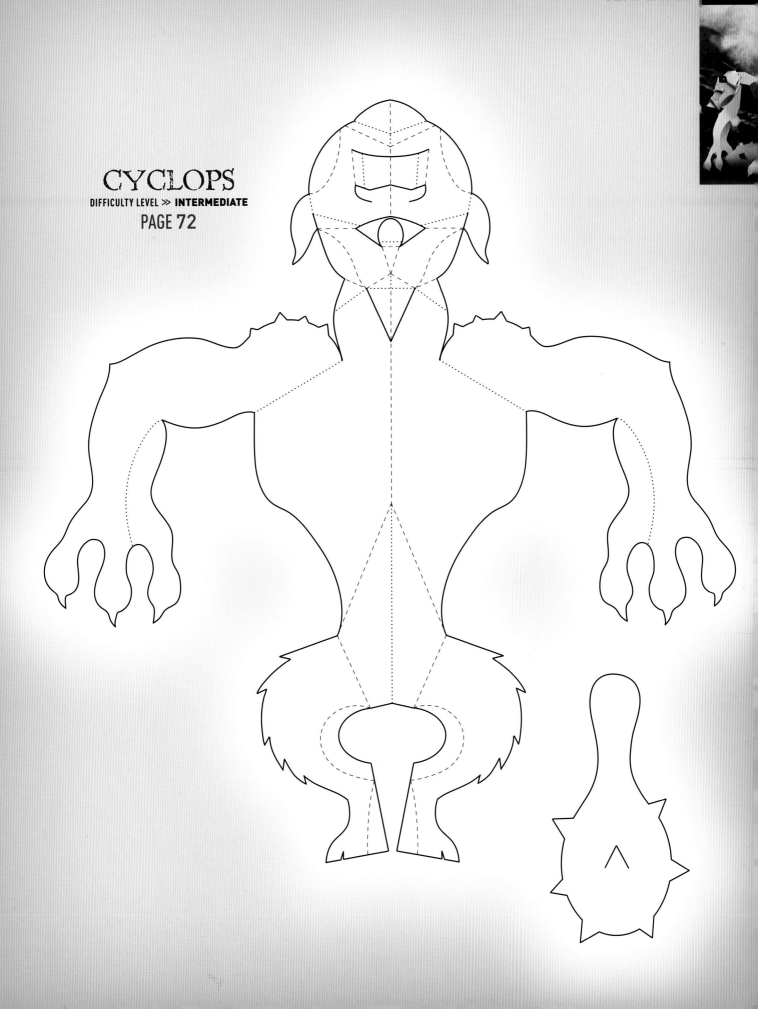

CYCLOPS
DIFFICULTY LEVEL ≫ INTERMEDIATE
PAGE 72

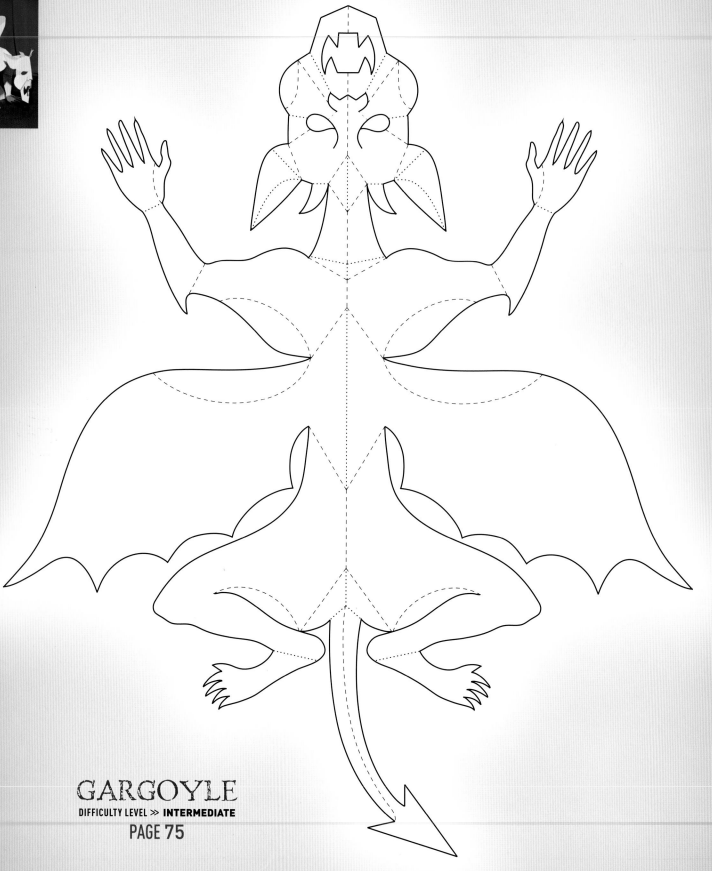

GARGOYLE
DIFFICULTY LEVEL » INTERMEDIATE
PAGE 75

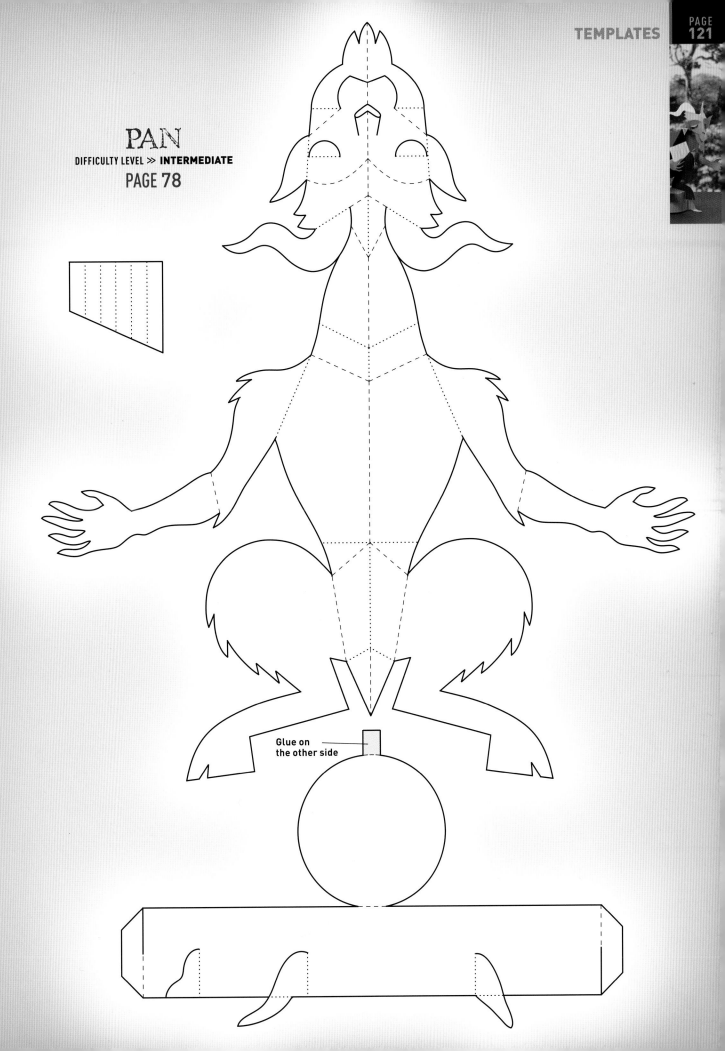

PAN
DIFFICULTY LEVEL >> **INTERMEDIATE**
PAGE 78

Glue on
the other side

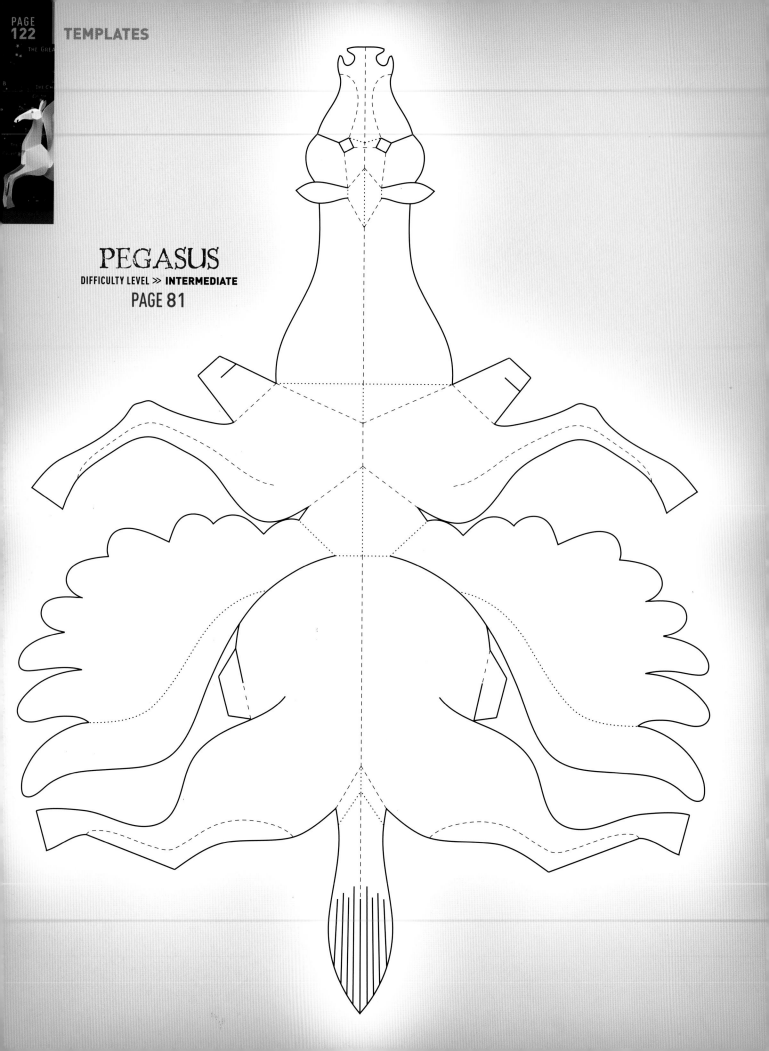

PEGASUS
DIFFICULTY LEVEL >> INTERMEDIATE
PAGE 81

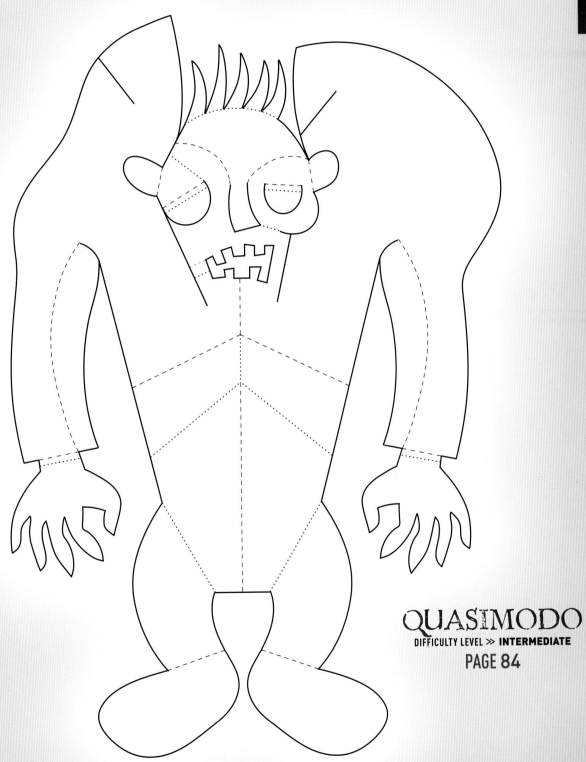

QUASIMODO
DIFFICULTY LEVEL >> INTERMEDIATE
PAGE 84

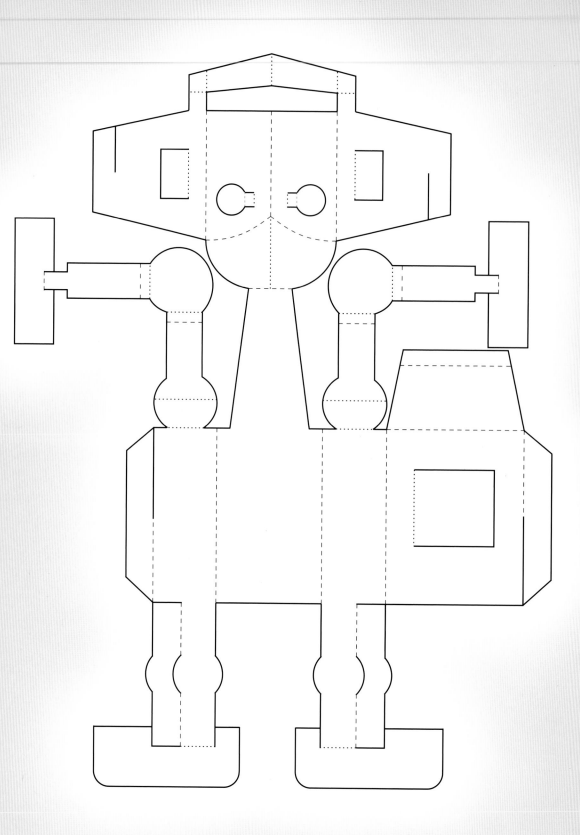

ROBOT
DIFFICULTY LEVEL >> **INTERMEDIATE**
PAGE 87

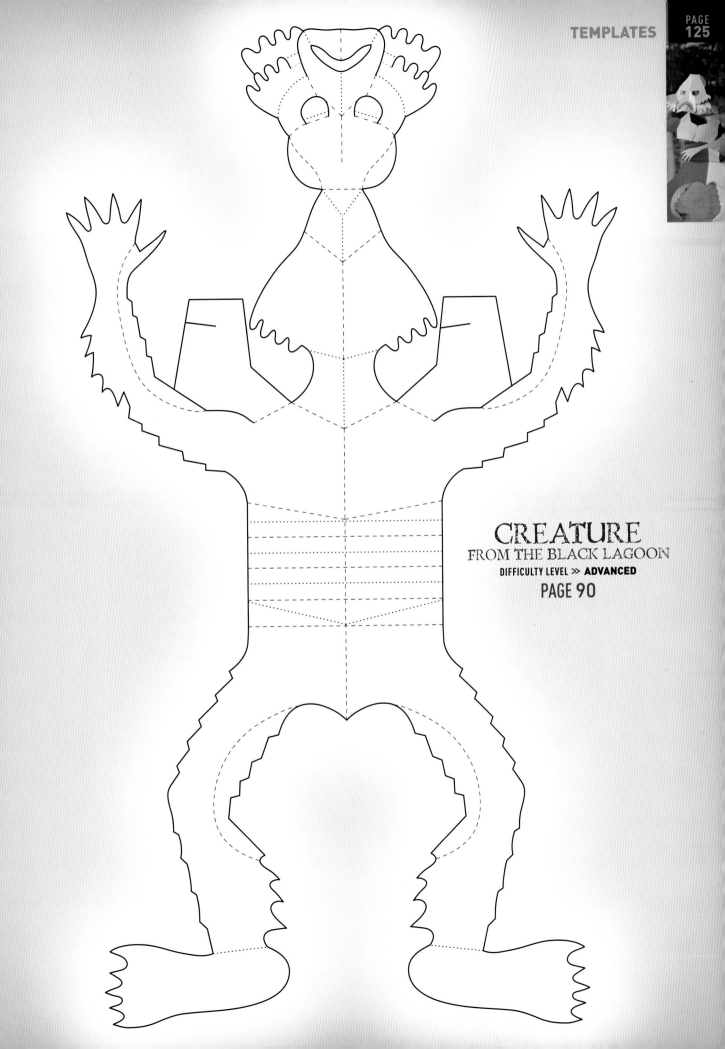

CREATURE
FROM THE BLACK LAGOON
DIFFICULTY LEVEL >> ADVANCED
PAGE 90

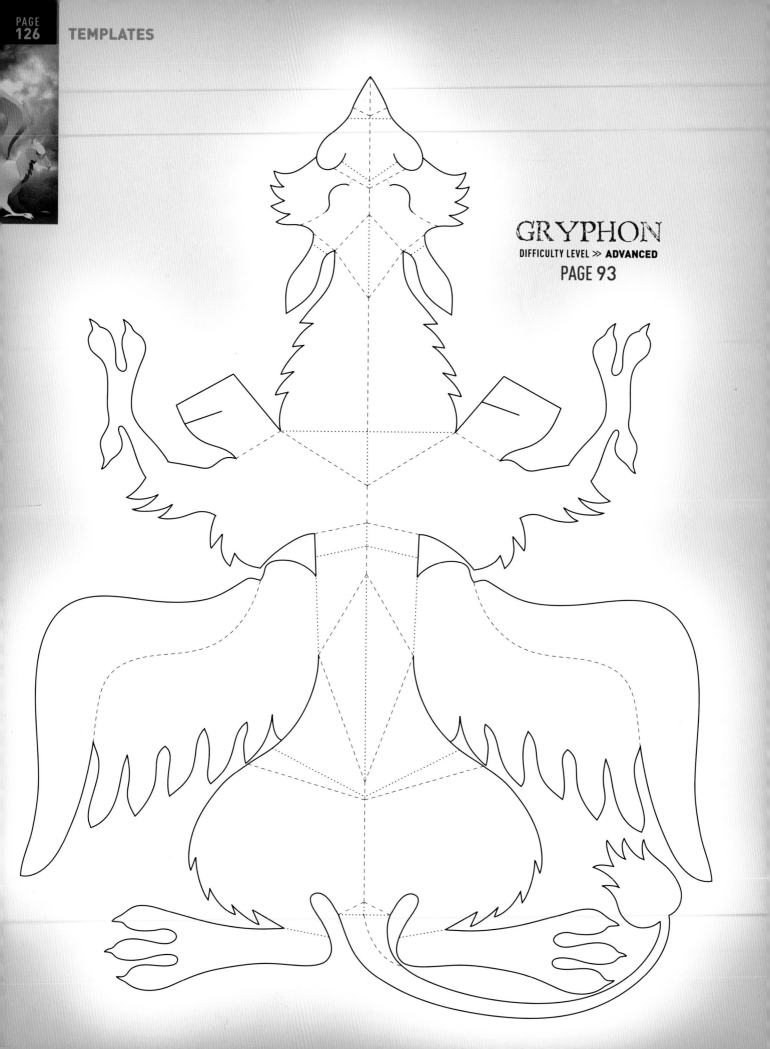

GRYPHON
DIFFICULTY LEVEL >> **ADVANCED**
PAGE 93